W
THE
O

THE WHO

& QUADROPHENIA

MARTIN POPOFF

contents

introduction

Quadrophenia's a tough nut to crack in The Who catalog. But then again, every damn album the band's ever made save for *Who's Next* (and, surprisingly, *Who*) has been the target of substantial carping and complaining.

Yes indeed, people love to go on about The Who. The first bunch of records in the 1960s are known more for their singles. Groundbreaking rock opera *Tommy* is pretty impenetrable, albeit accepted as an important part of pop culture at the time, especially when looked at as a package: record, film, soundtrack to the film, stage play, and a bunch of other permutations. There's also a beloved live album, *Live at Leeds*, chucked into the mix, featuring the band at its hard-hitting best. *Who's Next* is pretty much unassailable as an album and as a virtual greatest-hits collection of some of the band's loudest-roaring anthems. But to close out the 1970s, punctuated by the sad demise of Keith Moon, 1975's *The Who by Numbers* was carped about, as was 1978's *Who Are You*.

Lodged in the middle like a cyst, in a tired and tiring 1973, was *Quadrophenia*, The Who's second full-blown rock opera, the band's first and last album completely written by Pete Townshend. The record was designed to do a number of things, including celebrate the band's Mod roots, recapture the energy of that youthful time and place, and hopefully score another hit with a second sweeping concept. Roiling beneath were multiple forms of desperation, with Pete—through the very act of going back to work—striving to keep the squabbling team together, striving to keep the organization financially viable despite failing management, and striving to keep himself and Keith Moon from dying of the drink.

On top of all that, Pete was eager to keep the brand relevant. Curiously—and from the outside, sometimes furiously—Pete can be revisionist in all the intriguing and entertaining self-analysis he does in interviews. One particular crumpet of wisdom might fall into this category, but it's salient and worth mentioning: Pete says, annoyingly point-blank, that he saw punk coming. But then he finds himself tied in knots when he realizes that with *Quadrophenia*, ironically, he was making (and *had* to make) a progressive rock album, a double and a concept album to boot. Strangely, it was about punks, or more pointedly a subculture of proto-punks, and so to temper the artiness associated with prog rock albums, Pete at least put the story in the street—and in black and white, washed as such by overcast skies about to burst.

Still, dispensing with the time travel of the narrative for a moment, *Quadrophenia* in 1973 was viewed as merely another album by an establishment act, rock stars at the top. It was conceptual, to be sure, but never really considered or debated as part of the progressive rock canon. Nor could any of us see that the record would produce future currency (even if Pete said he saw it), although that's what it did; The Who served as one of the few dinosaur acts that retained its credibility with the punk generation of 1976 and 1977 and then again, sensibly, during the Mod revival of 1979.

But in isolation, in 1973, just like years before and after, *Quadrophenia* perpetuated the fine tradition of The Who putting out a studio album that people complained about. Fans eventually came around like they did with *Who Are You*, *Face Dances*, and to a substantial extent, *The Who by Numbers*. Out of all of those, *Quadrophenia* has arguably enjoyed the greatest rise in reputation, to the point where even the band, ambivalent about the results in the early years, went out on tour decades later and played the whole damn thing live, adding ambitious film footage to boot. Also decades later, reflecting more of an insidious validation and assimilation, was the rise of Oasis, Blur, and Britpop, representing a Mod revival that was more widespread but also less defined than the short, sharp, and shocking one of 1979—the sound is only partly there in 1995, owing much to The Beatles, but one can also spot parkas and the odd scooter.

As far as The Who is concerned, there are three clumps of Mod-ness that are important. Looking back to 1964, in the beginning there was Mod culture and The Who. As will be explained in the coming pages, The Who was important enough, over and above Small Faces and The Kinks, to be recognized as a cultural force in itself. In the last period, 1979, there was the *Quadrophenia* movie and soundtrack album, the Mod revival, and The Jam, who, during this time, deserves to be name-checked as fully half of the story to tell. In between the two periods stands 1973's *Quadrophenia*, The Who's sober, even-handed, ambitious, and lavishly appointed double album, a document that summarized what came before and then served as the first draft of the script of what came after.

This book celebrates all of this—the first wave and then the reverberations—in words and pictures. The album serves as the anchor, the biblical text, the distinguished work of art right in the middle temporally and conceptually speaking and therefore is the subject of the pages right in the middle of the book.

Then there's the wider context, including The Who before 1972 and what happened to the band after *Quadrophenia*. We've provided profiles of the group's infuriating early-days handlers, Chris Stamp and Kit Lambert. And we look at each of the guys in this remarkably human and ragtag band—Roger, Pete, John, and Keith—all wildly different from one another as people, the composite of each of their roles so odd against the expected and usual configuration of most rock 'n' roll bands. What results from this random, disparate grouping is a band that sounds like no other, one that defies categorization and splatters an organic, evolved 1973 Who-ness all over this much-debated double album instead of—it must be pointed out—Mod music to go with the Mod story.

And although *Quadrophenia* is much debated, there's a grounded sense of satisfaction in that any heated side-taking is in the nuance, the abstract, the mulling over of how creatively successful the record was and is. There's scant danger of getting hung up in the story itself or even the steady-handed music, both of which are earthy, understandable, and cause no distraction, nothing like *Tales from Topographic Oceans* or *Lifehouse* or even *Tommy*.

Indeed, the existence of myriad action points and cultural touchstones, but not particularly any anxiety over layers of meaning, resulted in the penning of this book being a joyful exercise for the author. In other words, the story of *Quadrophenia* itself, rather than the story within it, turned out to be wildly entertaining enough. It's not hard to imagine when Kit is bouncing checks, Keith is popping pills, and Pete is out on the river recording seagulls. But, of course, we will be looking at all of it, hopefully coming out the other end not only with a new appreciation for *Quadrophenia* but also perhaps a few lessons applicable to your own sullen but hopeful internal Jimmy yearning for more out of a life, one that I'll assume has moved well beyond the teenage years so artfully depicted by Pete across the songs on this questing journey of an album.

"Remember when stars were in reach"

1

← The Who at Duke of York's HQ in Kings Road, Chelsea, on November 12, 1966, while recording five songs for NBC TV. From left: Roger Daltrey, John Entwistle, Keith Moon, and Pete Townshend. Later that day they flew to Neuschnee, a village in Switzerland, for a four-day break. The car is a 1955 Volvo P1800 coupe.

They came from different frames of mind but the same place: Acton in East London. Stocky Roger Daltrey was there first. Expelled from school at fifteen, he rose from street gangs and a construction job into playing guitar with The Detours, a band he put together in 1959 when rock was still a toddler. John Entwistle was next, having transitioned from French horn to guitar (briefly) and finally to bass on account of his beefy hands. Roger had spotted "the Ox" on the street one day carrying a bass and recruited him into his act. John Entwistle suggested schoolmate Pete Townshend for the band; Pete had grown up in a musical family and was broadening his horizons at Ealing Art College.

Like the guys in The Beatles, The Rolling Stones, and The Kinks, Roger, Pete, and John, with Harry Wilson drumming and Colin Dawson singing, were inspired to the point of insanity by recent rock 'n' roll—there wasn't much of it—and its antecedents: blues, soul, and R&B. As would become a trend, the band increasingly drew inspiration from anybody and everybody making a splash locally. Johnny Kidd & the Pirates was of particular interest as Roger moved over to vocals and Pete became sole guitarist, handling lead and rhythm and blurring the space between them like Alan Caddy did in the original Pirates.

Into early 1964, given the existence of an act called Johnny Devlin and the Detours, the band decided on a name change, considering The Group, No One, and The Hair before settling on The Who. (Boss Roger made the final decision.)

← From left: Pete, Roger, Keith, and John—aka The High Numbers—getting Mod all wrong

→→ Maximum R&B: The Who performing on the TV pop music show *Ready Steady Go!*, London, 1965

↑ Pete smashes his guitar and amp at the Windsor Jazz & Blues Festival, Windsor Racecourse, July 30, 1966.

→→ Pete Townshend, the band's relentless creative force, at his London home in 1967

"REMEMBER WHEN STARS WERE IN REACH"

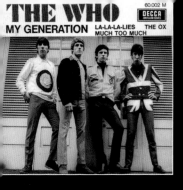

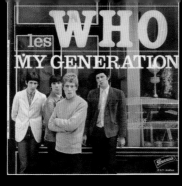

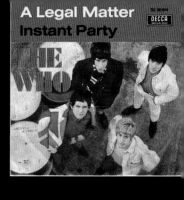

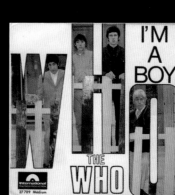

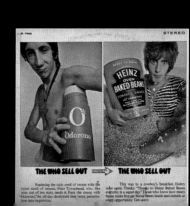

After firing its drummer, The Who was playing a gig with a stand-in when Keith Moon barged into the position and played a few songs, performing a sort of live audition. He passed due to his energy, having broken a drum skin and the bass pedal. Soon he left his own long-standing act, The Beachcombers, and dedicated himself to The Who full-time.

Strangely, two sets of managements had a go at slotting The Who into the burgeoning Mod music and fashion (and transportation) scene. First came Peter Meaden, who suggested a name change to The High Numbers, under which the guys recorded their debut single, "Zoot Suit"/"I'm the Face," for Fontana. When the single fizzled, the band changed its name back to The Who and got with a couple of filmmakers, Chris Stamp and Kit Lambert. In the process of trying to make a documentary about a fab new group, they became The Who's management team.

By this point, the band was deeper into R&B and soul music, calling it "Maximum R&B." The maximum showed up in the athletic stage set, where everybody but John looked fit to burst. The film situation didn't go completely wrong, with Stamp's and Lambert's efforts living on through the iconic short clip of the band playing the Railway Club. The clip demonstrates a sense of coming mania onstage and in the crowd, punk rock before punk, heavy metal before heavy metal, Mod culture emerging right before our eyes in visceral black and white, not quite fully kitted.

↑ Monterey Pop Festival, June 18, 1967, Monterey, California. Pete famously clashed with Jimi Hendrix over who would go on first and thus be the first to smash a guitar.

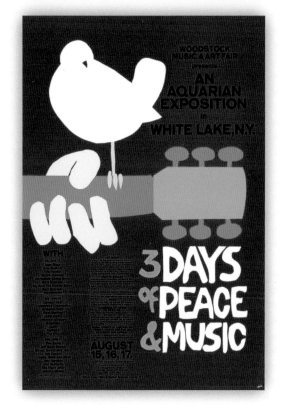

Next came a production deal with Shel Talmy and a hit song called "I Can't Explain," which Pete wrote to sound like The Kinks' song "All Day and All of the Night." The song reached #8 on the U.K. charts, aided by regular play on pirate station Radio Caroline and an appearance on *Ready Steady Go!* Follow-up single "Anyway, Anyhow, Anywhere" was a Top Ten success as well and was thereafter used as the theme music for *Ready Steady Go!* A #2 hit with "My Generation," featuring a stutter mimicking a Mod on pills, a firestorm of drums from Keith, and the famous line "Hope I die before I get old," transitioned into a debut album of the same name. There's John wearing a Union Jack jacket, and into the record, coming up behind "My Generation," is "The Kids Are Alright," another instant Mod classic.

Drama within the ranks increased, featuring power struggles and even physical fights between members and a litigious break with Shel Talmy, beginning what would become a lifetime of bad deals and subsequent financial disasters for the band. No matter how much an aggressive Roger tried to run a tight ship, dealing with Chris, Kit, John, and a pill-popping Keith was like herding cats, and Pete slowly but steadily became the creative force in the band, albeit sometimes at the expense of watching expenses.

Marbled among eventful single releases came a second and third album, *A Quick One* (called *Happy Jack* in the United States) and *The Who Sell Out*, the latter of which found the band in mind-expansion mode, assembling a sort of concept album where unrelated

songs were linked with fake radio ads in tribute to pirate radio. *A Quick One* included Pete's first foray into an extended narrative through a nine-minute song suite called "A Quick One, While He's Away," impressively ambitious for an album issued in 1966.

In between the two records, with Mod being declared over, The Who tentatively joined the psychedelic revolution, as evidenced by the band's stage attire at the 1967 Monterey Pop Festival, a historic stand at which Pete Townshend clashed with Jimi Hendrix over who would go on first and thus be the first to smash a guitar. The Who won that battle—the guys went nuts at the end of their sixth number, "My Generation." Amusingly, during the mayhem, members of the stage crew periodically swanned in to remove as much equipment as they could. A guitar definitely died in the battle, but it looked like everything else survived.

The ensuing U.S. tour supporting Herman's Hermits established the band's reputation for destroying hotel rooms, as Keith discovered that cherry bombs were a legal purchase. "I Can See for Miles" became a hit in the United States, with the band conducting further tour duties with Eric Burdon and the Animals. They also appeared on *The Smothers Brothers Comedy Hour*, their visit famed for its unexpectedly destructive use of pyro, too much of which was packed into Keith's bass drum. Once again, it was the conclusion of "My Generation" that signaled the beginning of the onstage riot.

WHO

SHRINE

PETER GREENS FLEETWOOD MAC

JUNE 28-29

THE CRAZY ARTHUR WORLD BROWN

THE ELECTRIC THEATRE CO.
PRESENTS AT · AARON RUSSO'S
KINETIC PLAYGROUND
4812 No. CLARK ST. — TEL: 784-1700

FRI · SAT. MAY 23-24	FRI · SAT. MAY 23-24	FRI · SAT · SUN. MAY 23-24-25
LED ZEPPELIN	PACIFIC GAS AND ELECTRIC	ILLINOIS SPEED PRESS
THURS · FRI · SAT — MAY 29-31	THURS · FRI · SAT · MAY 29-31	THURS. FRI. SAT. MAY 29-31 · SUN. JUN. 1
THE WHO	BUDDY RICH AND THE BUDDY RICH ORCHESTRA	JOE COCKER AND THE GREASE BAND · SOUP
FRI · SAT — JUNE 6-7	FRI · SAT · SUN — JUNE 6-7-8	FRI · SAT · SUN — JUNE 6-7-8
VANILLA FUDGE	MUDDY WATERS	ROTARY CONNECTION
FRI · SAT — JUNE 13-14	FRI · SAT · SUN — JUNE 13-15	FRI · SAT · SUN — JUNE 13-15
ERIC BURDON	THE ZOMBIES	IT'S A BEAUTIFUL DAY
FRI · SAT · SUN — JUNE 20-22	FRI · SAT — JUNE 20-21	FRI · SAT · SUN — JUNE 20-22
FEATURE ATTRACTION TO BE ANNOUNCED	CRAZY WORLD OF ARTHUR BROWN	THE YOUNG-BLOODS

DOORS OPEN 7:30 · CLOSE 3:00 · TUES - $1.00 LOCAL
TICKETS: FRI SAT $5.00 SUN $3.00 · TALENT - JAMS AUDITIONS
★ ADVANCE TICKETS ★
TICKET CENTRAL (212 N. MICH) - ALL WARD'S, FIELDS AND CRAWFORD'S
STORES - BOTH MAN AT EASE STORES - HOUSE OF LEWIS IN OLD TOWN
CHICAGO GUITAR GALLERY (216 S. WABASH)
★★★★★ EVANSTON: SPECTACLE HEADSHOP ★★★★★

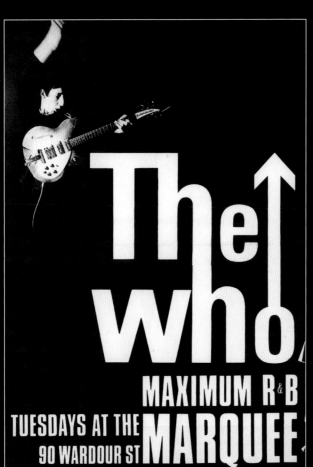

The WHO

MAXIMUM R&B
TUESDAYS AT THE MARQUEE
90 WARDOUR ST

18

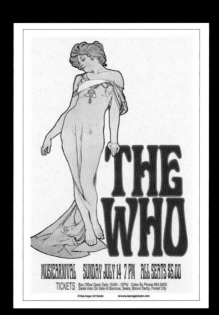

THE WHO

MUSICARNIVAL · SUNDAY JULY 14 · 7 PM · ALL SEATS $5.00
TICKETS

THE WHO

WEDNESDAY
JUNE 24

plus
THE JAMES GANG

Spectrum 8 p.m.

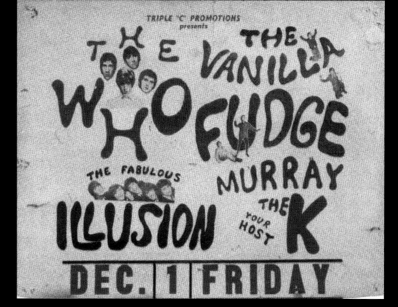

TRIPLE "C" PROMOTIONS
presents

THE VANILLA
WHO FUDGE

THE FABULOUS
ILLUSION

MURRAY
THE K
YOUR HOST

DEC. 1 FRIDAY

THE WHO
JAMES COTTON BLUES BAND
CARETAKERS
SANTA MONICA CIVIC AUD.
WEDNESDAY
AUG. 28
7-10 P.M.
TICKETS: $4.00
FREE PRESS or
BOOKSTORES DR.

BILL GRAHAM PRESENTS IN SAN FRANCISCO

THE WHO
LOADING ZONE
FILLMORE
JUNE 16-17

Domenica 26 Febbraio 1967
ore 16,30
PALAZZO DELLO SPORT

1° SUPER POP SHOW
presenta

The WHO

PATTY PRAVO · NEW DADA
THE BAD BOYS · THE PIPERS
THE BLACK STARS · The Primitives
DANY & GEPY · THANE RUSSALL AND THREE

presenta
GIANNI BONCOMPAGNI

PREZZI: PLATEA L. 1500 · TRIBUNA L. 1000
informazioni e vendita biglietti

After more worldwide touring, including a trip to Australia and New Zealand with Small Faces, the band tucked into the making of *Tommy*, conceptual at its genesis and then elaborately so; the project expanded into a double album with complementary and sometimes competing themes, featuring an overlay of Eastern mysticism due to Pete's adoptions of the teachings of Meher Baba. The album eventually emerged on May 17, 1969, and was an instant critical and commercial success, celebrated most iconically by the band's cranky Woodstock performance at 5 o'clock on Sunday morning, at which ungodly time they played most of the new album.

A show more satisfying to the band at a festival on the Isle of Wight was next, followed by the *Live at Leeds* album. The limited track selection—heavy, jamming, and half old rock 'n' roll covers—was designed to show how savage the guys could rock. It was a sharp contrast to the ponderous, proto-prog rock expanse of *Tommy*, which incorporated substantial acoustic guitar along with quite clean and uneffected electric guitar, not to mention piano and vocal harmonies. "Young Man Blues" and "Summertime Blues" were proto-heavy metal standouts from the live album, which the band followed up by issuing a strong non-LP studio single called "The Seeker."

By this point, the individual personalities in the band were so distinct and pronounced that each member was a sort of cultural touchstone on his own. At the rhythm end, there was John, the stoic music-headed technician with a dark sense of humor, set against Keith, the flailing, mad-eyed drummer. Pete, now increasingly philosophical and really leading the rock community into deeper thought along with John Lennon (and before them, Bob Dylan), had taken to wearing one-piece boiler suits, making his quirky proto-new wave stage moves all the more arresting. Up front, Roger was coming into his own as a singer and "actor" of Pete's songs, with his bare chest and long, curly blond hair setting the template for the golden god front man, soon to be extrapolated upon by Robert Plant.

Tommy and *Live at Leeds* would both certify as gold records in the United States almost immediately, with The Who now as big as anybody at the turn of the decade. But then came the descent of both Kit Lambert and Chris Stamp into substance abuse and the resulting bad management of the band's in-house label, Track Records. Everybody was suddenly getting on everybody else's nerves, and spending was frivolous and wasteful.

Despite all this, the guys managed to rally with an album now widely considered to be the best Who album of all time. *Who's Next* drew some of its power from the fact that it's a compromise between the band members over Pete's plans for a complex and conceptual follow-up to *Tommy*. *Lifehouse* was supposed to explore the relationship between band and audience, a concern of Pete's surely seeded way back with his invention of onstage "auto-destruction," stemming from the first time he smashed a guitar. But his Eastern religious views were part and parcel of the project as well, as were Sufi mystical teachings and ideas around sound, vibration, and collective consciousness.

Despite Pete suffering a nervous breakdown over the album's failure to launch, a pile of musical groundwork had been established leading into what's next: *Who's Next*. Eight of the nine selections (save for John's "My Wife") evolved onto the record from the *Lifehouse* project, with the Glyn Johns–produced record generating several hits and enduring rock radio classics, including "Baba O'Riley," "Bargain," "The Song Is Over," "Going Mobile," "Behind Blue Eyes," and finally, "Won't Get Fooled Again," the band's anthem for the ages, situated at the end of the record and punctuated with a Roger Daltrey scream that portends ensuing trauma. At this point, The Who wasn't so much a band running on fumes but more like one parked at the station, getting gassed beyond full, petrol sloshing and spraying everywhere while the pumper takes no notice and smokes a cigarette.

→ Roger declares victory at the Théâtre des
Champs-Elysées, Paris, January 16, 1970.

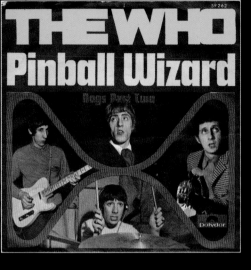

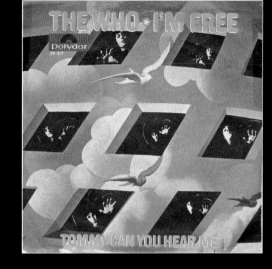

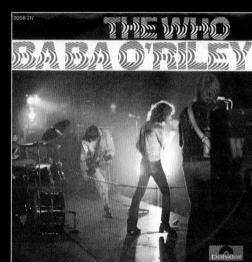

↑ German tour poster, 1972

↖ Keith at Tara, his home in Chertsey, Surrey, in 1972 with his daughter, Amanda (left), and some of the cars in his collection, including a damaged Ferrari Dino

On *Who's Next*, specifically and immediately with "Baba O'Riley," Pete pioneered the use of synthesizers and, more impressively, sequencing and looping, adding additional fresh synth sounds to "Bargain," "The Song Is Over," and "Won't Get Fooled Again," the latter of which features the second celebrated and groundbreaking loop on the record. This would be further explored on *Quadrophenia*, as would the band's regular use of acoustic guitar and piano. In addition, *Who's Next* might mark Keith's apex as a drummer, but some of the craziness on display here carried over to *Quadrophenia* as well.

But that's getting way beyond The *Who's Next* cycle temporally (at least in amped-up Who time) and most definitely psychologically, for here things are happy and all about seething energy. Come the next record, The Who experienced somewhat a sense of ennui, world weariness, and attendant physical degradation. Conversely, back in 1971, *Who's Next* represented all four of the guys at their peaks: Pete writing concisely but still thoughtfully, Roger hollering with power, and the guys in the engine room feverishly shoveling coal into the furnace with no regard for what the temperature gauges are reading.

Sensibly then, the album went gold immediately, eventually certifying at triple platinum in the United States. Touring dates in support of the album were also hugely successful, beginning in the United States in July 1971 and then transitioning to home soil in September, followed by a return to the United States, finishing up in Seattle on December 15, 1971. Also to be further explored during the *Quadrophenia* cycle, the band played "Baba O'Riley" and "Won't Get Fooled Again" to a prerecorded synthesizer backing track. What followed the tour was the longest break the guys ever took (eight months), after which nobody returned particularly rested—restless, more like, just as frazzled and burnt at the wick as if they had started on the next record the day after touching down at Heathrow.

MODS VS. ROCKERS

Modernist. That was the term used in Colin MacInnes's 1959 novel *Absolute Beginners* to describe a new type of younger jazz fan, one that listens to the modern jazz of Charlie Parker and Dave Brubeck as opposed to traditional jazz. To go along with the fresh take, these fans also dressed sharp, adopting some of the styles from the artists they liked as well as Italian fashion and beat culture.

And then on it went—ready, steady, go!—evolution in all directions. At the music end, jazz made way for the rhythm and blues and soul records brought over by American servicemen stationed in the U.K., as well as Jamaican ska, introduced through immigration. Then the kids started making their own derivative or second-wave music, with The Beatles being key, then The Rolling Stones, Small Faces, The Kinks, The Yardbirds, and The Who, along with less prolific acts like The Action and The Creation.

At the fashion end, kids took pointers from French and Italian art films and started getting their suits tailor-made, accented by thin lapels and thin ties, eventually shrouded in parkas. Dark sunglasses made you look thoughtful and brooding. Female Mods were all business with a sober androgynous look—slacks and page-boy haircuts—but they then got into shorter and shorter miniskirts and shiny boots, which transitioned smoothly into the look carried over into the psychedelic era. Later, the adoption of the Royal Air Force "roundel" logo as well as the Union Jack helped define the composite as something distinctly British.

The idea with the fashion was summed up in a line from The Who's first manager, Peter Meaden (a card-carrying Mod), who called it "clean living under difficult circumstances." Because even if Mod culture came out of the cities, from middle-class Jewish kids in London's East End and beatniks solving the world's problems late into the night at coffee bars and listening to music on jukeboxes (which often included sides brought in by customers), it was street level. The general theme was to project oneself aggressively as a station or two above what a tedious clerk job in a shoe store might suggest, to be defined instead by one's high-minded taste in music, film, and fashion and not by the drear of daily postwar circumstance working for the man. There was also a whiff of ironic appropriation in it as well, an embrace of commercialism and materialism—of grown-up kit—when a kid shouldn't be looking and acting that way.

Literally getting any self-respecting young Mod the hell away from the boss took a scooter, preferably a Lambretta or a Vespa. These affordable Italian machines, often bought on payment plans, were also easy to park and worked well with the hours Mods kept, given that public transit closed down way earlier than a Mod night out necessitated. They also allowed the Mod to escape the cramped quarters of the city center on trips to seaside towns, where he'd wind up in well-documented rumbles with Rockers, considered rough and uncultured with their love of traditional rock 'n' roll, yesterday's music.

➔➔ Nattily dressed Mods wearing suits and parkas pose with scooters covered with extra lights and wing mirrors, Peckham, May 7, 1964

↑ A pair of Rockers astride their motorcycles, October 24, 1963. Rocker fashion was antithetical to Mod fashion in obvious ways.

Antithetical in every way, Rockers were also boozers, as were old people (parents). This went against Mod culture, with sharp teens adopting amphetamines—"purple hearts"—as their drug of choice. First, uppers were legal (although often stolen in pharmacy break-ins), but there was a certain sense of pride in going opposite, enhancing alertness and embracing experience, rather than rounding off the edges of the workday at the pub with a jar or two. The effect was that these natural music aficionados could dance into the early-morning hours, learning about more obscure American music by the hour, soaking up more and more "maximum R&B," before dashing off on their scooters—festooned with multiple rearview mirrors and headlights, the name of the owner maybe written on the windscreen—and then dragging themselves dead to life into the shop a few hours later to deal with customers.

But Mod scooters soon became a symbol of violence, a product of the aforementioned clashes between Mods and Rockers. Rockers, with their motorcycles, greased hair, and leather jackets, looked at Mods as effeminate. Rockers tended to come from the country and up north, ergo they were usually kept away from the Mods, who congregated in London and the home counties of wider London.

But then came the run-ins, which all made the papers. The first of these "moral panics" was in Clacton, overblown, followed by Margate, Hastings, and Southend. Most notable was the Battle of Brighton Beach on a church holiday known as Whitsun weekend, May 18 and 19, 1964. (Usually there's talk of these things happening on various "bank holidays" because that's when everybody was off work and could travel.) Brighton Beach is considered the central event in Mod lore, crystallized in *Quadrophenia* the film, if not overtly the album. Various instances of "getting the boot in" moved up the coast to Hastings, with many arrests made. But it was more so the lurid news reports and accompanying pictures that had clergy and politicians up in arms that such displays of hooliganism were going to British society.

With the clashes subsiding after 1964, purists figured the golden era of Mod culture was over. Adequately convincing Mod clothes could be bought off the rack, resulting in wannabes. A scooter now singled you out as a pill-popping ne'er-do-well. A date for the shuttering of the scene is hard to discern, but then again it's also quite difficult to tell when or how it had all kicked off, given that it was an underground movement and a subtle—even tasteful—one at that. Arguably it only becomes definitive when we get Mods making their own derivative music, records (ironically) tailor-made by Mods for Mods. In this respect, 1965 and 1966 are the height of Mod as a package of fashion, sound, and transport. It is in this apparently near post-Mod environment that the heroes of our story, The Who, came to define Mod music. And, by way of the profile of the band in sound and moving picture, it was music first and foremost that took over as the defining feature of Mod culture.

← These photos from 1965 (left) and 1964 (right) provide a contrasting view of later-period Mod and Rocker styles. →→

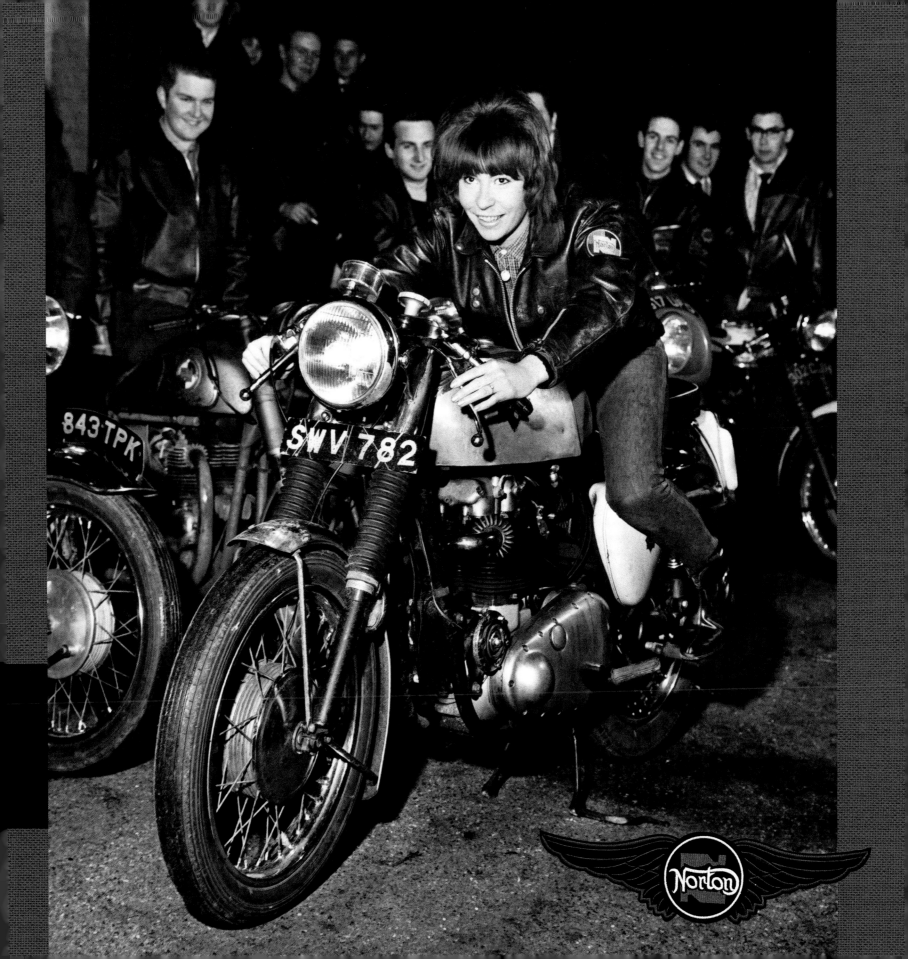

"The fifth and sixth members of The Who" is how Roger described Chris Stamp and Kit Lambert (both no longer with us), the management duo that turned the band into a sharp cultural statement with guitars before contributing significantly to the near implosion of the group in 1973 due to exhaustion, drug habits, and looming financial ruin.

Chris Stamp was a working-class East End Londoner, a tugboat captain's son turned filmmaker. (The most famed of the five Stamp siblings was actor Terence.) Kit Lambert was Oxford-educated and the only child of composer Constant Lambert and actress Florence Kaye. Constant left the family home due to an affair with a ballerina in his company and then died at the age of forty-five, causing Kit an anguished childhood. Kit then became a British Army officer and embarked upon an expedition in the Amazon in which one of his two colleagues, Richard Mason, was killed by an indigenous tribe.

Together Chris and Kit were, as Keith perceptibly saw it, a team as incongruous as the members of The Who, completing a six-man sack full of cats that barely held it together over ten years of frenetic, shouting, boozy partnership. Chris, a roustabout and lady's man, spoke heavy Cockney, and Kit, gay, multilingual, and an epicurean, spoke high-society English. Their manner and mannerisms personally affected the roles they played when trying to control The Who and point them approximately in a forward direction.

Chris and Kit had already worked on a few films together out of Shepperton Studios, usually as assistant directors. Kit soon found himself checking out The Who at the Railway Club and was transfixed by the band's effect on the crowd, who had been sort of stunned into submission as they watched each personality on that small, low stage do something very different from the next. At Kit's behest, the two cooked up the idea to create a film about a zeitgeist-defining pop band. Although no feature-length film emerged, the guys wound up managing the band, usurping Peter Meaden, who, it was discovered, had no legal claim on the band and subsequently agreed to a buyout.

It was Chris and Kit who prompted the name change from The High Numbers back to The Who and further refined the band's Mod image. Kit was more the visionary, encouraging the onstage violence and pushing the use of volume to extremity. Kit also became the band's producer, collaborating closely with Pete, whom he encouraged to write grandly and fearlessly, buying him two Revox tape recorders so he could work at home.

Along with coaching the band on its stage image and coming up with the idea that the guys should own their own lighting, in 1966, Chris and Kit established a record label. Track Records famously signed Jimi Hendrix and Arthur Brown (along with Thunderclap Newman, Fairport Convention, and Golden Earring) but also issued many Who singles along with the albums *The Who Sell Out*, *Tommy*, *Live at Leeds*, *Who's Next*, and *Quadrophenia* and compilations *Meaty Beaty Big and Bouncy* and *Odds & Sods*, a final contractual obligation album in 1974.

Part of the motivation for the label came out of the desire to work with Hendrix, but part of it was to allow The Who more creative freedom. As it turned out, signing with Shel Talmy and working with his contacts at the Decca and Brunswick imprints turned out to be a source of grief. Chris and Kit were not entirely successful breaking their deal with the notorious impresario. After being sued by Ed Chalpin in the United States, who laid claim to a dodgy management deal with Hendrix, Track was quickly thrown into further financial turmoil.

↗↗ Chris Stamp (left) and Kit Lambert (right) at the offices of Track Records in Soho

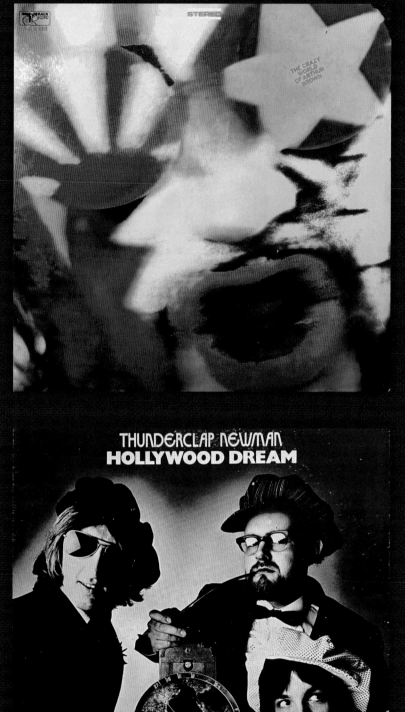

↗ Lambert and Stamp issued albums by Golden Earring, Thunderclap Newman, and Arthur Brown, among others.

Still, the hits kept coming, and Track managed to hold on to Hendrix in the U.K. His success, along with that of The Who, allowed for lavish personal spending, with Kit and Chris paying themselves 40 percent of the band's gross. Despite their generous restitution, there were further financial improprieties, soon exacerbated by heavy drug use by both comanagers (somewhat caused by Keith, who was the guilty party that introduced Kit to pills).

When the odd couple was operating properly, it was Chris's job to be the mover and shaker and the wheeler-dealer, sometimes using strong-arm tactics and always cutting corners, keeping creditors at bay. Conceptually, his main concern was promoting the band in America, with a late triumph being getting the band resigned with MCA in the United States for $750,000 per album. Kit was there to think big and, in his role as producer, think orchestrally, notably inspiring Pete to combine rock with opera, resulting in *Tommy*, the first hit album for the band.

Due mostly to Kit's boozing and now three-year heroin habit and resulting bleeding of the coffers (in truth, all six of them were to blame for the spending of what Keith called "mad money" or "madness money"), the band, at the behest of Roger and then John, audited and subsequently broke with Kit and Chris. Replacing them was Bill Curbishley, who over time has become one of the most respected names in the business and is still managing The Who to this day. Another breaking point with Kit had to do with him shopping a film version of *Tommy* without the band's consent, although, truth be told, Pete specifically was in favor of a film happening.

However aggravated he was, Pete still believed in Kit (as did Keith), enlisting him to help in a sort of executive production role on *Quadrophenia* before realizing his heroin habit had made him basically ineffective and untrustworthy. At one point, Kit wrote a huge check to the band and put a stop on it the next day, fleeing to his Palazzo Dario villa in Venice. In January 1977, The Who settled its disputes with Chris and Kit. Pete received $1 million and the band collectively gained back its copyrights from "Substitute" forward through *Quadrophenia.*

With Kit and Chris eventually relocating (fleeing) to New York, Track continued to operate, issuing product by Johnny Thunders and the Heartbreakers and Shakin' Stevens. It then folded in 1978 before being revived by manager Ian Grant in 1999.

After the demise of Track Records, Chris stayed in New York. His drug and alcohol issues carried through to 1987, at which point he entered rehab and got clean. He eventually became a therapist using a psychotherapy approach known as psychodrama, also obtaining certificates in a number of other counseling areas, including acupuncture and drug and alcohol dependency. He died from cancer on November 24, 2012, at the age of seventy.

Kit died on April 7, 1981, from a brain hemorrhage after falling down the stairs at his mum's place. The fall was the final tragedy suffered by the destitute and already gravely injured Kit, who, according to Pete, had been beaten up the night before in the washrooms at a gay club in Earl's Court, apparently by a coke dealer over unsettled drug debts.

"You only see what we show you"

[THE SESSIONS]

2

Leading up to the *Quadrophenia* sessions, the parts that made up The Who had never been more disconnected. Worst for wear was Keith, addled by booze and pills and enabled by Stamp and Lambert, who were in not much better condition. To bide his time during a quiet 1972 for the band, Keith had acted in a movie called *That'll Be the Day*, starring Rosemary Leach and rockers David Essex and Ringo Starr. Taking the role served as a metaphor for a man entering alcohol-induced paranoia over his real job. Keith had lost confidence in his abilities and would show up to the studio late and drunk, convinced the sessions would go badly and then fulfilling the percussive prophecy.

Adding to the contrast, both John and Roger had spread their wings through the construction of solo albums. In fact, work on *Quadrophenia* was delayed as the lead singer finished up *Daltrey*, issued in April 1973, the same time as Keith's film. Over at the low end, John had issued a second solo effort, *Whistle Rymes*, in November 1972, just as The Who was managing to record a few new songs with Glyn Johns producing, most pointedly "Is It in My Head?," "Love, Reign o'er Me," "Long Live Rock" (a mini suite), "Join Together," and "Relay." The latter two would be issued as non-LP singles right away. "Join Together" scored a #9 placement on the U.K. charts while managing only #17 in the United States. "Relay," issued in the fall, and backed with the instrumental "Waspman" from the same sessions, did even worse business.

Pete had considered the clutch of new material not enough of a progression from *Who's Next*, but inspired by the mini opera, he found himself moving in the direction of what would become *Quadrophenia*. To do the project properly, Pete figured the band needed its own studio. A company called Ramport was formed, which in turn purchased a decommissioned church in Battersea, South London, for £15,000. Work then began on what originally was called The Kitchen, soon to be Ramport Studios.

←← Keith in *That'll Be the Day*, 1973

↑ Amsterdam, Netherlands, August 17, 1972

Renovation of the facility moved along swiftly but at great cost: £330,000, by Pete's estimate. It was an enormous sum in 1972, and ironically is an enormous sum for a studio today, given advancements in technology. Still, it wasn't finished in time (a fire over the Christmas season of 1972 didn't help), specifically lacking a workable mixing desk. Ronnie Lane's mobile studio—LMS—was brought in to rescue the day, and the facility had to be changed from eight-track to sixteen-track over the course of a weekend. Pete—always first there and last to leave—indisputably produced the finished record, but aiding greatly were engineers Ron Nevison and Ron Fawcus, who ran the mobile outside via camera linkup. The arrangement was quite advanced for the day, but it turned out to be a bit of a farce because the band was regularly competing with construction crews. The Who would record something and then in the lulls allow the builders to bang away and vice versa. Nevison recalls that recording the band was easy, except miking Keith's drums was a nightmare given how many pieces he was using. Pete provided clear direction for most every detail, stemming from the assured direction of his demos.

Making the project more difficult was the attempt to record the album in quadraphonic sound, a technology still in its infancy but coming along thanks to the groundwork laid by Alan Parsons over at the sessions for *The Dark Side of the Moon* in late 1972. Although the title of the new project would suggest a record dominated by this technical theme,

THE WHO & QUADROPHENIA

"quadrophenia" was more a modification of the term "schizophrenia," referring to the idea that the Jimmy character of the narrative possessed a composite personality reflective of the four members of The Who.

Complicating matters further was the prodigious use of synthesizers; Pete's time-consuming Arp 2500 parts were constructed in his home studio and then patched in. (Pete would travel between studio and home on the Thames using a motorboat; Roger was unfortunately stuck with a two-hour drive each way.) Pete and Nevison contributed further with remote recordings by getting out and taping seagulls, waves, and traffic, along with a train whistle, captured near Pete's house at Goring-on-Thames. Back at the studio, nine tape decks had to be set up to capture all the sounds that needed blending on "I Am the Sea." In addition, Pete learned to play the cello and violin well enough to multitrack together modest string parts.

Pete also insisted on composing the entire *Quadrophenia* rock opera but intentionally left his demos skeletal to allow substantial input from Roger, John, and Keith, whose recorded performances were done more so in isolation than in the past. There was also the matter of John's laboriously assembled horn arrangements, which added to the complexity of making an album in an unfinished converted church studio with a mobile Airstream trailer.

↑ Roger in the recording studio set up in a barn at his home, Holmshurst Manor in Burwash, East Sussex, November 23, 1972

↑ Live performance of *Tommy*, the Rainbow Theatre, London, December 19, 1972

Pete's monastic May to June 1972 demo sessions were followed by further work in April at Mick Jagger's Stargroves house near Newbury in the Berkshires. Jack Adams and Kit Lambert produced these sessions, and Pete surmises that some of the backing tracks might have been carried forward onto the album. The official *Quadrophenia* sessions commenced at Ramport on May 21, 1973. There were still problems with the Helios mixing desk and the sound in Pete's cube-designed control room, so work carried on with the Lane mobile until early July, when the issues with the Ramport control room were resolved.

Outside of these hurdles, Ramport was a joy. The guys had a bar set up in a flight case near the piano booth, and they played configured as they would be onstage and at considerable volume, with Keith's drums in front of a large window that allowed light to stream in. Unusual for the day, there were three isolation booths for ensemble recording of delicate bits, as well as all manner of exotic instruments purchased from Manny's in New York and piled up at the back of the hall, most of which were never touched.

As for the control room, augmenting the blue Helios desk was a selection of brand-new Studer and 3M recording equipment, allowing the band dependable access to twenty-four-track recording and beyond. Usually there were two to four speakers as monitors in a control room, but Ramport had twelve JBL 4320s, creating a sound Pete describes as "monstrous," certainly the case when one pressed the cheeky "Do not press" button, which let off the sound of a nuclear explosion at 138 decibels.

↑ Pete on his boat on the River Thames, Richmond upon Thames, London, April 1968. During the mixing of *Quadrophenia*, Pete picked up Ron Nevison daily in his boat.

↖ Keith, October 1973. Note the two rows of tom-toms.

← The Ox with his Thunderbird bass, February 1975

← Pete appears in Eric Clapton's Rainbow Concert at the Rainbow Theatre, London, January 13, 1973. When he's not busy with the maracas, he's playing a Gretsch 6120 Chet Atkins.

With respect to the band's gear, Keith used a black Premier kit, distinguished from his previous setup by a second row of toms. His heads were Premier Extras and his cymbals Paiste. John used various Gibson Thunderbird basses, chiefly a mahogany-bodied IV, changing his output for *Quadrophenia* to Sunn Coliseum power amps and a Stramp preamp to cut back on his signature bright, trebly sound.

At the synth end, Pete used either his Arp 2500 or Arp 2600, recording all his synth parts at home, which by necessity would be the case for most of the band's synth parts on other albums too. As for guitars, his main weapon of choice was his orange 1959 Gretsch 6120 Chet Atkins Hollow Body, which had already gotten a good workout on *Who's Next* and would be used for virtually all of Pete's Who and solo studio sessions up through his *Psychoderelict* concept album of 1993. On "I Am the Sea," "Quadrophenia," "The Dirty Jobs," and "Doctor Jimmy," Pete used a 1957 Stratocaster. For acoustics, he went with either his 1968 Gibson J-200 or twelve-string blonde Guild F512-NT.

Mid-June found the band with basic tracks recorded already for three or four songs. The guys were still oscillating back and forth between the Ramport control room and the remote as they recorded vocals and Chris Stainton's piano parts. By June 28, they were listening to studio mixes for most of the album. Also ready was non-LP gem "Quadrophenic Four Faces," which appeared on the soundtrack album of the movie as "Four Faces." On July 2, work in the mobile continued until late at night transferring five of Pete's eight-track demos to new sixteen-track masters, resulting in usable bed tracks. The following day, the guys listened to more session mixes, after which Pete recorded his lead guitar work on "Bell Boy." July 5 was taken up with horn over-dubs—Pete says this was the last day that

Lane's mobile was used. Additional brass work took place on July 6 and 11. Pete completed more leads over the next few days, including "Drowned" and "Dirty Jobs," also playing organ and piano.

After a weekend off and a short Monday of vocal work, on July 17 the guys played with some of the more exotic sounds on the record, including flugelhorn, timpani, anvil, gongs, and emulated foghorn sounds worked out by John, who also handled additional brass overdubs. Pete says he always enjoyed working in the studio with John, who'd be relaxed and in storytelling mode. With Roger, it was all about efficiency—get in, get singing, and get out.

Pete had the studio to himself on July 24, and he played violin to be used on "I've Had Enough" and "Love, Reign o'er Me" as well as guitar parts for "5:15." Pete also worked alone two days later, playing guitar and adding vocal harmonies. On this day he had Tony Haslam do some tap-dancing for a sound effect sequence. On the 27th he was alone once again, recording his guitars for "The Real Me." Roger then worked for fully six hours on the 28th on various vocals.

July 31 was a momentous day—Keith turned in his uproarious and affected "Bell Boy" vocal. This represented some proper levity with respect to Keith, who otherwise was cause for all manner of concern. Pete was annoyed that Keith constantly tried to cadge money off of him (as was Lambert, his manager!). He regularly showed up to sessions inebriated and usually with some girl he had picked up, even though he professed to be in anguish over the failing relationship with his wife, Kim. Roger did some singing, and the band then kicked back to listen to the results thus far, well and pleased and in a celebratory mood. As part of the boozy meeting, it was deemed that "Four Faces" and "We Close Tonight" would be dropped from the track sequence.

← Pete strums his Gibson J-200 at rehearsals for the stage version of the band's rock opera *Tommy*, at the Rainbow Theatre, London, December 9, 1972. Like the Gretsch 6120, it would figure prominently in the recording of *Quadrophenia*.

↑ The Who's other Swiss Army Knife, France, 1972

→ Pete used either his Arp 2500 or Arp 2600 (shown), recording all his synth parts at home.

← Pete using portable recording equipment on the banks of the River Thames with his father Cliff Townshend. Pete's field recordings played an important role in the album's soundscapes.

The next day was spent preparing the tracks to be sent to Pete's barn studio at Cleve, Goring-on-Thames, where Pete and Nevison would mix the double album from August 3 to September 12, adding significantly to the off-location late hours spent in Goring constructing Arp parts. Nevison stayed at a bed-and-breakfast across the river, and Pete picked him up every day in his boat.

Pete's plan was to get a stereo mix done as well as a quad mix. But then he was hit with the news that the stereo mix of the album was slated for an October 13 release date (to catch the Christmas selling season), with the tour to begin on the 28th. Already feeling guilty due to excessive time spent away from his family, Pete had to give up the dream of creating a quad version of the album. A further complication came when Pete deemed the U.S. label's version of the quad to be a farce, essentially stereo slightly altered through trickery. Much to MCA's consternation, Pete refused to go with the plan. Preparations for the live show were rushed, resulting in technical snafus once the band hit the road, ill-prepared and still exhausted from making the record.

Famously, Pete had gone forty-eight hours without sleep preparing prerecorded tapes to be used in the show, technology that was still in its infancy in 1973. Showing up at stage rehearsals in Shepperton with his work, Pete was told by Roger that he had waited long enough and wanted to go home. Pete flew into a rage and took a swing at him with his guitar, after which Roger knocked him out with one punch. Everybody was at wit's end, and to boot, *Quadrophenia* was way over budget, Track Records was about to go broke, Chris, Kit, and Keith were a mess, and (most important to Pete) Pete wasn't going to get the two or three weeks he needed to finish his masterpiece properly.

↑↑ Keith joins a demonstration to demand a children's crossing on Thessaly Road in London, August 16, 1973, near the group's studio in Battersea.

↑ Having some fun in their Highgate home are Keith, his daughter Mandy, and his wife Kim, December 26, 1974.

John was never happy with the final sonics of *Quadrophenia*, specifically when it came to his bass parts, which he considered too low in the mix. He also thought that there wasn't enough dynamic range from soft to loud in the composition and arrangement of the songs—something also pointed out by George Jones, who mastered the album at the Mastering Lab in Los Angeles. Fans were quick to point out that Roger's vocals also suffered (Roger groused about this too, calling them thin because of the echo Nevison added to his voice) and that Keith's drumming ranged from unimaginative to sloppy on the rare occasions he tried to be the old Keith. In defense of the mix, Nevison said that the speakers weren't great in Pete's studio and that there weren't enough tracks to accommodate everything, especially with all the sound effects. Creating the crossfades was also time-consuming, given all the edits. He conceded that equalization had to be added to give the album more top end and that extra work was done in mastering.

It's hard to agree with any of the complaints. Or at least as these things go, it's hard to agree with any of this until someone points it out and the listener studies his or her way through the album focused on a single complaint at a time. In other words, it's somewhat fruit-bearing as an academic exercise, yielding a measure of validity in some areas more than others. As far as this writer goes, I'd cop to there being a sense of relentless density during certain stretches and then at the end in composite. As for these other quibbles, I wouldn't have noticed them had I not been directed to consider them.

↑ Pete was too busy to join the boys when they received a gold record award for *Tommy* in London, February 28, 1973.

W hile all rock operas are concept albums, not all concept albums are rock operas—that's the first distinction. Ergo, there are many more concept albums than rock operas.

The definition of concept album is comparatively broad, roughly referring to an album made up of songs with similar themes, the critical mass of them revealing a larger, more complex theme. Woody Guthrie's 1940 album *Dust Bowl Ballads* is often considered the first concept album, and Frank Sinatra enters the discussion as well. But more adjacent to The Who, *Sgt. Pepper's Lonely Hearts Club Band* is cited as the first concept album of the rock era, along with The Mothers of Invention's *Absolutely Free*, strangely issued on the same day back in 1967. *Pet Sounds* by The Beach Boys also gets the nod, but so do the heroes of our tale with *The Who Sell Out*, due to that album's insertion of fake commercials suggesting a pirate radio station theme, although the songs themselves are unrelated to each other or to the radio station theme.

Things heat up when we get to *S. F. Sorrow* from Pretty Things, issued in December 1968 and based on a short story by vocalist Phil May about a character called Sebastian F. Sorrow. The record squarely qualifies as the first rock opera, even if that term is problematic from the onset, given that, historically speaking, there haven't been any operatic vocals in a rock opera (occasional comedic Frank Zappa bits excepted). Instead, the idea is that the song cycle from a rock opera could easily enough be adapted to stage or film, with characters in the songs singing their thoughts. There's usually a strong sense of chronology and narrative and multiple action points, making for a story through music and vocals—essentially what an opera is. To address a couple of finer points, rock operas don't necessarily pay lip service to the plot and theme tropes that characterize most iconic conventional operas, but on a more abstract level, both operas and rock operas are accused of evoking a degree of melodrama and self-importance, attracting a measure of ridicule.

Moving forward in time, The Who in fact had to defend itself from accusations that the making of *Tommy*, issued on May 17, 1969, was influenced by the critically acclaimed song suite by Pretty Things. Then there's The Kinks, who dabbled in the conceptual pre-*Tommy* and, also in 1969, issued its magnificent rock opera *Arthur (Or the Decline and Fall of the British Empire)*. (In 1975, The Kinks released another rock opera called *Soap Opera*.)

And then in 1973, within the same temporal and geographical space as iconic concept albums like *Thick as a Brick*, *The Dark Side of the Moon*, *Tales from Topographic Oceans*, and *The Lamb Lies Down on Broadway*, Pete Townshend crafted *Quadrophenia*, The Who's second rock opera. The band and management were fine with the new album being deemed as such, given how *Tommy* had triumphed by this point as the greatest album ever within the limited classification. *Quadrophenia* was literally a case of The Who making a follow-up rock opera to *Tommy*, and no one within the band or outside of it bristled at the identifying term. Then *Quadrophenia* proved its mettle as such through a clearly articulated story, augmented in the enclosed booklet by what served as stills from an as-yet-unrealized movie. Then, of course, six years later there *was* the movie, which stuck close enough to the record without much problem, another clue that *Quadrophenia* was a rock opera.

By the way, The Who album was not "prog rock" in any way, save for the inclusion of a few fussy instrumental bits. The Who was squarely a 4/4 band with the occasional 3/4 time signature, and there were no egregiously long songs. To be sure, a deeper

analysis would reveal that the band's bass player did more (and more oddly) in a conventional four-minute rock song than Yes bassist Chris Squire did across the expanse of "Close to the Edge" or "The Gates of Delirium." But overall, The Who wasn't wired like that, even if the guys in Rush adored them, indeed considering The Who, Cream, and Led Zeppelin all to be progressive rock bands. What's more, the story of Jimmy and the Mods was regular to the point of banal, lacking in the exotic spirituality, centuries-deep historical sweep, or paranormal occurrences of a typical prog rock album.

Still, illustrative of how the rock opera can be the subject of derision against the more sober idea of the concept album, Pink Floyd's *The Wall* could sensibly be called a rock opera, while *The Dark Side of the Moon*, *Wish You Were Here*, and *Animals* would be deemed concept albums and nothing more. Taking the next step, it's fairly supportable that each of those are considered greater works of art than *The Wall*, which, in the spirit of opera, perhaps blubbers and blabs on a bit too obviously (with cheap laugh-level spoken word bits and sound effects to match) compared with the more oblique and thoughtful concepts and subconcepts expressed by Roger Waters on the three records previous.

Switching back to The Who, one can't help but think that *Who's Next*, *The Who by Numbers*, and *Who Are You* are considered by many to be more serious works of art than *Quadrophenia*. Indeed, even the much-lauded *Tommy*, the most famous rock opera of all time—film, stage play, symphonic version, you name it—is probably appreciated more so for its smash singles in isolation versus any literary merit attached to the tale of Tommy Walker, which is, frankly, kind of creepy. Such is the curse of the rock opera, which seemed doomed to derision the minute it was given that preposterous name.

3

"Can you see the real me, can you?"

← Keith and Pete collaborate on a kerranging chord, circa 1973.

I AM THE SEA

And here begins our track-by-track analysis of The Who's double helping for 1973. Like a rocker's unbeknownst impression of a typical opera, *Quadrophenia* opens with bad weather, torrents of it. "I Am the Sea" is mostly the work of Ron Nevison, who took the mobile to Perranporth Beach in Cornwall to capture waves, in quadraphonic in fact, using four U87 microphones, although only the stereo got used. For the ubiquitous rain on the track, Nevison recorded in Wales and right outside of Ramport Studios. The hoped-for thunder never happened, so that was lifted from an archival recording.

Massaged into the background are snippets of music, first a sweeping and atmospheric piano performance and a hollering Pete, but then briefly a horn line (representing Roger's theme song, "Helpless Dancer"), "Is it me, for a moment" (representing John's theme, "Is It Me?," nestled into the song "Doctor Jimmy"), "Bell boy" (Keith's theme), "Love, reign on me" (Pete's theme), and finally "Can you see the real me, can you? Can you?" before a seamless transition into "The Real Me."

The end effect of this setup to the tale is one of intrigue, along with confusion on the part of the listener and, as we'll find out, mental anguish on the part of the story's protagonist, Jimmy, who is being tormented by the different components of his personality. These competing personas are represented by the members of The Who, and all four themes are sampled, rattling around in his brain, distant, echoing, reverberating from somewhere just beyond the line of vision in a dark and stormy sea.

↘ Phil Daniels, who starred as Jimmy in the 1979 film, is decidedly less tormented than his character as he enjoys a bite with Pete during a break from filming.

↓ Ron Nevison used four of the popular U87 microphones to capture the bad weather that opens "I Am the Sea."

Also, as we'll later ascertain, the device represented by "I Am the Sea" is one of reflection, a waking at the end of what was already a waking dream. It's close to the end of the story with Jimmy in the depths of despair before what we see on pages 40, 41, and 42 of the booklet found in the original vinyl, where one hopes that Jimmy's head is now playing Nevison's bits from the opening track and none of The Who's bits. Perhaps he is no longer quadrophenic, but still, as the title suggests, he is the sea, a concept that adds a further level of complexity along the lines of Pete's own Eastern religious questing. Not only has Jimmy been purified through waves and rain drowning out the voices in his head, but he's possibly cognizant that he belongs to something larger that makes him simultaneously connected to the universe and infinitesimally insignificant, which is more than okay—it's ecstatic.

↑ Sporthal de Vliegermolen, Voorburg, Netherlands, March 10, 1973

Can you see "The Real Me" Can you
The Who

THE REAL ME

Next up is the most famous song on *Quadrophenia*. "The Real Me" features everybody in The Who doing what they're known for: John is up the fretboard interpolating and extrapolating, Pete is playing what may as well be bass lines on wiry rhythm guitar, Keith is dancing frantically somewhere between snare drum and hi-hat with regular escapes down through his toms, and Roger is hollering the words to a punk rock anthem before there ever was punk rock. Come chorus time, braying horn arrangements do their best to nullify the combat rock purity.

For the elongated third verse section in the middle, Roger's singing is done entirely over bass and drums, and marbled throughout is a profusion of clanging jamming. The last verse offers yet another surprise: Roger is backed by what is basically a full-blooded, riffy heavy metal band, or at least something like MC5 on a tear. What's more impressive, apparently John recorded his triumphant bass part for the song in one take, stating in a 1996 interview that he was just joking around—which makes sense, because despite the virtuosity and the regular dashing off of unexpected licks, his performance is somewhat comedic. It's also very different from what Pete did on his October 1972 demo of the track, which is quite elaborate and funky in all directions, like Motown.

At the lyric end, Jimmy is going through the struggles of teen identity but at least seems to be open about his problems. But elders aren't helping. His mother tells him it runs in the family, his "shrink" won't let on what he thinks, and the local pastor seems to get spooked by Jimmy's anger and shows him out. In addition, his girlfriend has given up on him, but we don't learn why.

There's also a sense of paranoia, exacerbated by pills ("leapers"), with the paving stones in the street causing hallucinations (or at least anxiety). In the windows of the row houses around him, peering out are strange people who know him. In other words, he can't relate to them, but they've figured him out, another manifestation of paranoia. At the end, the music dissolves and Roger calms down a bit, singing "Can you see the real me?" one last time, only the "me" echoes quickly and jarringly, underscoring the existence of multiple personalities within Jimmy.

"The Real Me" was issued as a single in the United States and Canada, backed with "I'm One." Japan put the rare "Water" on the B side while France and Belgium paired it with "Doctor Jimmy." "Water" had been recorded in May 1970 while Pete was recording the Thunderclap Newman album *Hollywood Dream* in his home studio. Also recorded at that time were "Postcard," "Naked Eye," and "I Don't Even Know Myself."

The European releases were picture-sleeve singles, while the North American versions weren't (significantly, there was no U.K. issue). The song went on to become a regular live favorite for the band. The most notable cover of the song was by W.A.S.P. on that band's *The Headless Children* album from 1989—Blackie Lawless is a big Who fan and often features busy Keith Moon–style drumming and general Who-like cacophony across his band's heavy metal songs. W.A.S.P. made a video for the track, which got to #23 on the U.K. charts and features on a couple of live albums by the band.

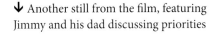

↓ Another still from the film, featuring Jimmy and his dad discussing priorities

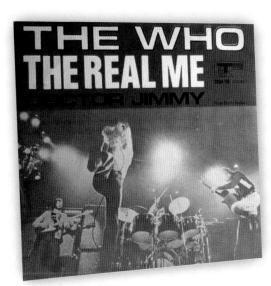

→ The instrumental title track finds Pete, among other things, soloing cleanly like David Gilmour.

↓ Pete was an early adopter of synthesizers, including the ARP 2500, which he endorsed.

QUADROPHENIA

Track three, an instrumental called "Quadrophenia," begins with vigorously strummed "Pinball Wizard" acoustic guitar, piano notes, and Pete soloing cleanly. Keith checks in with a bold fill, and we're off into a hard rock passage structured around a chord sequence that feels like something John would write. At the forty-second mark we get a dissolve, with Pete continuing to solo over a melancholic mellow bit and then a regal bit, pomped and tarted by synths and a blustery Keith. Then there's a key change and a languid second dissolve. Synths percolate along virtually alone for a spell, and then the band strikes up again through a bit of a renaissance arrangement followed by a "Happy Jack" bass vibe and then a raga jam of sorts. Cue a third dissolve followed by a new theme, with solo piano opening to a second early visit to "Love, Reign o'er Me" (a good minute of it), followed by a big windup and a return to ocean wave sounds. Along with "The Rock," we get all four themes in alternate interpretations, an idea already explored at a subconscious level or even a state of hypnagogia through opener "I Am the Sea."

"Quadrophenia" represents hours and hours of toil by Pete working at home, bouncing tracks between two tape machines, playing the role of electronic-era classical composer, making judicious use of his Arp 2500. As Townshend noted, Keith's drums replaced his placeholder drums, John's bass replaced his bass, and Pete might have added a bit more guitar, but the rest of this suite was created in his home studio. As presented, the composition runs over six minutes, and being instrumental and sequenced as what is really only position two on the album, it risks erasing any sort of forward momentum, especially in contrast to the hepped-up James Brown-isms of "The Real Me." On the other hand, it upholds the album's credentials as a rock opera, a progressive rock album, a symphonic rock album, and a concept album.

↑ Though the title track represents hours of toil by Pete on every instrument,
John's bass (and Keith's drums) replaced Townnshend's demo tracks on the final.

↑ Sporthal de Vliegermolen, Voorburg, Netherlands, March 10, 1973

→→ Our befuddled protagonist's humanity comes through in "Cut My Hair" when he admits he's pretty sure he won't be living at home much longer given that his mom found a box of "blues" in his room.

CUT MY HAIR

Next, "Cut My Hair" was one of the first songs Pete wrote for the project, and as he explains, it's the first that puts Jimmy in a Mod context, given that the two earlier written tracks were "Love, Reign o'er Me" and "Is It in My Head?" The key identifier is "zoot suit, white jacket with side vents five inches long," which Pete borrowed (and slightly expanded) from "Zoot Suit," written by manager and Mod Pete Meaden for The Who when they might have become The High Numbers.

The structure of the track is sufficiently up to snuff for a rock opera, featuring a melodic soft rock verse, followed by an amped-up chorus driven by Keith practically soloing, abdicating his assumed role as timekeeper. Pete sings the verses while Roger features on the aggressive chorus. Late in the sequence, there's a (double) key change for what one might call a break, which given the hectic beat (snare on one, two, three, and four), as Pete has noticed, jives nicely with the idea of Jimmy on "leapers." Then we're back to an altered arrangement for another verse, which ends Pink Floyd–like with "found sounds" in the background, in this case, the radio and a whistling kettle.

Our befuddled protagonist's humanity comes through when he admits his dad is an okay guy, even if Jimmy's pretty sure he won't be living at home much longer given that his mom found a box of "blues" in his room—again, more humanity in that Jimmy's admitting he's probably going to be sent away rather than stomp out on his own accord. Elsewhere, the internal debate is all about fitting in and how hard it is to keep up appearances as a Mod. At the end of the song, he returns home on the first train in the morning, missing his dad, who has just left for work. The final image is of Jimmy's fried egg for breakfast making him sick, although we don't know if it's from the previous night's substance intake or from disgust at how routine his nights and crashed mornings have become.

← Roger Daltrey and Phil Daniels relax in Brighton during a break from filming, early 1979.

←← Pete in another capture from Voorburg, 1973; note Roger in the background in his distinctive, iconic "marching" mode.

THE PUNK AND THE GODFATHER

Closing side one of the record is "The Punk and the Godfather," originally called "Punk in the Gutter" (but referred to simply as "Punk") and then further rejigged to "The Punk Meets the Godfather" for the U.S. release of the album. All told, it's a clanging, action-packed Who rocker, featuring verbose and wildly entertaining bass from John, roiling drums from Keith, power chords from Pete, and a big vocal up top by Roger, who harmonizes with himself. For the surprisingly pastoral section that serves as the chorus, Pete turns in a processed, high falsetto vocal, mockingly aping "My Generation." He sings the more conventional break as well, and like Roger does on the verse, he harmonizes with himself, turning in one of the most impactful Pete passages on the record.

Then we're back to the big-stadium rock chord sequence, only now there's ecstatic crowd noise adding further propulsion to Keith's machine-gun drumming. There's another verse and then finally another incident of Pete's haunting, almost faerie-like "m-m-my g-g-generation" refrain.

"The Punk and the Godfather" is much more of an ambitious and oblique lyric compared with the two quite baldly narrative banks of words that came before. Pete hints in "I'm One" that Jimmy is a frustrated musician, and there's an echo of that here through the amount of introspection he displays. But the main idea is that he's a next-level music fan that sees himself reflected in The Who, although he's not exactly the biggest fan. Really that makes sense because he's not all that much a fan of himself either. He's cagey enough on music to see the band's strengths and weaknesses, and he sees through the fame and realizes that

much of rock 'n' roll legend-making is based on lies. What's more, the band onstage just seems another branch of Mod culture, not necessarily leading it. In fact, it might not be that important over and above the kids in the crowd, who are, pointedly, a few years younger and therefore should be subordinate. Pete's also been known to expand beyond what's in the lyrics, saying that Jimmy goes to see the band and then plans to meet them as they leave the venue, only to be told, "Fuck off." In the end, a dismayed Jimmy is throwing rock 'n' roll on the pile of things that aren't contributing sufficiently to the rich and meaningful life he's seeking.

There's a bit of an incongruous time slip that the listener has to deal with here, for The Who portrayed in the lyric sound like The Who of 1973, not 1964. This also happens inside the booklet, where the band mugging for a photograph in front of the Hammersmith Odeon is also the current-day rendition, cleaned-up post-hippies as it were.

To summarize, *Quadrophenia*'s first side covers a lot of ground. We've got an atmosphere-establishing sound collage serving as an introduction to all four sides, a long and expository instrumental suite, and a smart, well-constructed progressive rock song in "Cut My Hair"—granted, it's performed Who-style, which is almost as anti-prog as punk is. Wrapping up, in "The Real Me" and "The Punk and the Godfather," we have two songs that are two of the most rousing and impression-making rockers from the entire record. But if it feels like a substantial number of Who tropes have been checked already, fasten your seat belts, because there are plenty more to be celebrated across the following three sides of the album.

B efore the curious Who fan could get home and tuck into the music enclosed, he or she had the bus ride back from the shop, upon which the *Quadrophenia* graphics in all their explanatory glory could be perused.

Beginning with the front cover, we are presented with an artful, subtle, black-and-white photograph generated from an idea by Roger and taken by Graham Hughes, Roger's cousin. Pictured is a twenty-year-old lad called Terry "Chad" Kennett—he's since died, in 2011—whom Pete had spotted in a pub on Thessaly Road near the studio and thought might be a suitable Jimmy, the protagonist of his Mod coming-of-age saga. Kennett turned out to be a colorful choice indeed. While in the employ of The Who, he was charged with stealing a bus and had to be vouched for in front of a judge so he could resume his duties being photographed for the booklet.

Back on the job (much to the relief of The Who), Kennett is pictured on a classic Vespa Gran Sport scooter, with his back to us. Hughes remembers having to "drive" the scooter up a staircase to his studio to create the shot, which was set against a sky-blue canvas. Drawn crudely on the back of Jimmy's Mod parka is a Who logo (Roger's idea), with the arrow pointing at his head. One might conjecture this serves as a metaphor for one of Pete's subplots to the story, the idea that Jimmy's "quadrophenic" personality is a composite of the members of The Who, a band he quite fancies. This concept is made fully graphic by having each of the guys' faces reflected back at Jimmy in the four rearview mirrors to his right. Hughes achieved this by having each of the band members crouch with his face reflected in the mirror. Keith wasn't around and had to be photographed in his greenhouse at home on his Tara estate. What results is a tidy representation of the idea that Jimmy sees Pete, Keith, John, and Roger when he looks at himself in a mirror.

Further underscoring the four-part conceit, we don't see Jimmy's face on the cover. And as we'll find out, in Mod terms, he's definitely not one of the "Faces," and given the prominent 113 license plate in the shot, alas, Jimmy is no more than a "Number" or "Ticket." The smoky softness Hughes applies to the iconic black-and-white shot suggests that we are looking back in time and falsely glamorizing what it was like to be a working-class teenager in 1964.

Over to the back cover, we get an ominous shot of Jimmy's scooter in the water, letting the potential buyer of the record know that enclosed is a story not without drama. In effect, although we don't know it yet, the scooter serves as a bridge between Jimmy's life onshore and his life being stranded on the rocks, reached on a stolen boat. The story will end ambiguously, with the listener not knowing to what extent this might have been a suicide attempt, and indeed, whether it was a successful one. Or perhaps it was rather something of a soaking-wet triumph, after which Jimmy might return to shore cleansed of his dependence via his identity as a Mod.

Inside the standard gatefold jacket of the original vinyl, on a fairly empty seashore background, there are some standard album credits on the right, but to the left, Pete offers a summary of the tale, stylized roughly to approximate Jimmy's voice. (He was inspired somewhat by Holden Caulfield in J. D. Salinger's *The Catcher in the Rye*.) Pete's aim with this abstracted summary of sorts was to flesh out the character's personality beyond what we get in the lyrics, pointedly getting across that he was an uneducated bloke but a decent guy at heart.

But the real triumph is the enclosed booklet, art-directed and shot in 35mm by American photography icon Ethan Russell, with much help from Who associate Richard Barnes. Page 2 and page 43 present the lyrics, while the front cover gives us an unadorned shot of council row housing and the

QUADROPHENIA

← The real triumph of the album's packaging is the enclosed booklet, art-directed and shot in 35mm by American photography icon Ethan Russell. Here we see the front and back covers.

back cover, sea and rocks. Pages 3 through 42, however, read like stills from a movie lost to time. Across the narrative, painstakingly assembled over thirty days of shooting and involving meticulous casting and costuming, we see Jimmy grimly living out Pete's story practically song for song, beginning with a shot of him cruising down the very street on which Ramport Studios is located. In the background we see Battersea Power Station, famed for its depiction on the cover of Pink Floyd's *Animals* album of 1977.

Elsewhere, we see Jimmy with his disapproving mum and dad and at his job as a garbage man. As Pete reveals in his introductory essay, his pay is set at nine quid, but he lasts only two days, collecting two quid. His coworkers ruminate over striking for more pay but are too indoctrinated to do so. He's also seen vandalizing a car with his buddies (part of this shoot was Pete's younger brother, Paul, very recognizable as a Townshend) and eyeballing wistfully his heroes (each with a girl on his arm) as they pose for a picture in front of the Hammersmith Odeon. Incidentally, this latter picture was taken on August 24, 1973, the same day that Hughes had conducted his shoot for the front cover of the album.

Things take a dark turn halfway through, as we see Jimmy sitting by his crashed bike and then sleeping off a long night of dancing and pills beneath the display of naked girl pictures in his room. Flipping forward, we see him trying in vain to fit in pretty much anywhere, shot alone and brooding in various locales (including the boarded-up West Pier in Brighton), reflecting and not coming up with answers. Then we see him leap into the ocean and commandeer a stolen boat. Aghast, we are presented with a picture of him seemingly drowned (they quickly discovered that the real-life Kennett couldn't swim), but then—turn the page—here's Jimmy walking ashore.

The narrative tour-de-force on display behind these professionally composed photographs perhaps made the eventual filming of Pete's story inevitable. And even if that wouldn't happen for six more years, the sum total of these pictures—along with Pete's long essay and his strong-on-plot lyrics—made following along with the story pretty much effortless. Indeed, as the project was taking shape, there had been a fear (mainly voiced by Roger) that hiring a West Coast American photographer to portray what being a Mod was like in 1964 London might turn out tone-deaf. But it was through Russell's professionalism, along with the stewardship of Barnes (who made sure that everything was authentically Mod and spared no cost in that pursuit), that the photo essay turned out as realistic as it did.

Peter Dennis Blandford Townshend was born on May 19, 1945, in Chiswick, West London. Family life was harsh, with his fighting, heavy-drinking, musical parents driving Pete toward survival through escapism. Adventure stories, rock 'n' roll, the movie *Rock around the Clock*, and attendance at a Bill Haley concert pointed him potentially toward life as a musician, although Pete claims that what he really wanted to be was a journalist. Pete was twelve years old when he got his first sibling, Paul, followed three years later by Simon, who later would be good for a half-dozen solo albums of his own, also joining The Who as touring guitarist in 1996.

At Acton County Grammar School, Pete formed his first band, The Confederates, which also featured John Entwistle on bass. Next came courses in graphic design at Ealing Art College, where Pete studied alongside the likes of Ron Wood before leaving the program in 1964 to concentrate on rock 'n' roll full-time.

By route of The Detours, we get The Who. Pete served as guitarist, primary songwriter, and secondary vocalist. He wasn't the leader in the beginning but soon took over by dint of his curious and capable intellect. With The Who, there'd be all those records written by Pete and then pierced by his quick-witted guitar work, both electric and acoustic, augmented by his pioneering use of synthesizers. But that wouldn't be enough. Between *Who's Next* and *Quadrophenia*, Pete would issue a first solo album called *Who Came First*, a sort of consolation prize for *Lifehouse*'s failure to launch. And then between *The Who by Numbers* and *Who Are You*, he'd issue *Rough Mix*, part of a duo with Ronnie Lane from The Faces.

But then came a creative solo-career breakthrough on the back of a near mental breakdown. Married since 1968 and with two kids, Pete had long since chipped away at this island of stability through the chaos of life in The Who. He'd nursed close friend Eric Clapton through heroin addiction, only to lose Keith Moon to an accidental overdose. His own substance-abuse issues (curiously not extending to psychedelics due to the teachings of Meher Baba but most definitely manifesting in a full-time dance with the drink and later, briefly, heroin) had Pete on the ropes. And yet, as his productivity would suggest, through the haze and desperation, he was more in love with the arts than ever.

On April 21, 1980, Pete delivered a creative triumph called *Empty Glass*, and Pete Townshend the solo artist began to eclipse the mothership, much to the consternation of Roger Daltrey, who had begun to grouse that Pete was sandbagging his best songs. As proof of the conspiracy, *Face Dances*, issued a year later, wouldn't be as strong as *Empty Glass*. *It's Hard*, issued in September 1982, also wouldn't be as strong as *All the Best Cowboys Have Chinese Eyes* (which had preempted the second Who album of the Kenney Jones era by three months).

Empty Glass spawned a couple of big hits in "Rough Boys" and "Let My Love Open the Door," with the album reaching #5 on the Billboard charts and certifying platinum. *All the Best Cowboys*—this writer thinks it's Pete's masterpiece, but it was rejected by critics of the day as pretentious—managed a #26 placement on the American charts and did not reach gold. With another Who album nowhere in sight and not to emerge until 2006, Pete rebounded in 1985, scoring another gold record with

→ A smartly dressed Pete Townshend, December 1967

WHO CAME FIRST

PETE TOWNSHEND   EMPTY GLASS

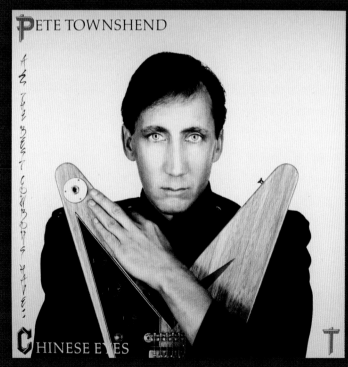

PETE TOWNSHEND

ALL THE BEST COWBOYS HAVE CHINESE EYES

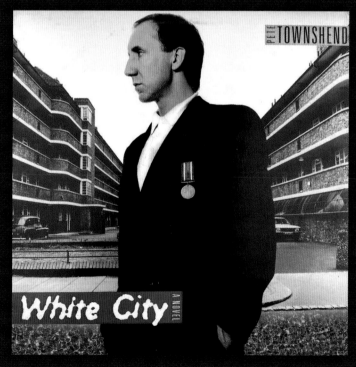

PETE TOWNSHEND

White City A NOVEL

← *Rough Mix* with Ronnie Lane of The Faces was a masterful effort that also featured John Entwistle, Eric Clapton, and Charlie Watts.

White City: A Novel, featuring hits in "Face the Face" and "Give Blood." *The Iron Man*, a 1989 concept album based on a story by poet and close friend Ted Hughes, fared less well critically and commercially, as did 1993's *Psychoderelict*, which marked Pete's return to rock opera.

In a parallel life and yet one that lines up so well with what Pete did for The Who, Pete became an actual author, most notably delivering a short story collection called *Horse's Neck* in 1985 and then a first-rate autobiography called *Who I Am* in 2012. He also signed on as an acquisitions editor for Faber and Faber in 1983, editing a number of rock 'n' roll titles as well as working on a collection of speeches by Prince Charles. All the while there have been essays, book reviews, scriptwriting, and novellas, not to mention thorough and insightful liner notes penned for rereleases of his own records.

Pete's later years featured a divorce in 1994 from his wife of twenty-six years, Karen; a new long-standing relationship with classical orchestrator and solo artist Rachel Fuller; residence in various English manor homes; and significant work in support of charitable causes. And how might we sum up Pete's creative life across all these years following the death of Keith? If one might be so bold as to apply some math to it, it's been one part new Who music, two parts hitting the road and playing the hits, and perhaps most pointedly, one part creating a solo canon that rivals anything he's ever done with Roger, John, and Keith—*Tommy*, *Who's Next*, and *Quadrophenia* included.

4

"I hear the music of a heartbeat"

← Roger enjoys a break during rehearsals, October 24, 1973.

→ Pete with a Martin acoustic, Twickenham

→→ Phil Daniels as Jimmy, in the iconic shot used for the front cover of the 1979 *Quadrophenia* soundtrack album

I'M ONE

Quadrophenia's second side opens softly with folk music. Pete is singing delicately to acoustic guitar with occasional sighing steel guitar sounds sent in that direction through volume control fades. But after a minute, he's joined by John and Keith, who take "I'm One" partway toward standard Who rocker. Only partway, however, because although Keith is amusingly off to the races, John plays a novel but structured and repetitive bass line and Pete only slightly turns up the vocal intensity, doing a sort of half-rocking Roger. (As it turns out, the underlying rhythm of the drumbeat is actually more interesting as played by Pete on his demo version of the song, where he puts the emphasis on the "and" of one, using bass drum and open-then-closed hi-hat, accompanied by a lingering bass guitar note.) The guitar work continues in the country frame of mind established earlier, with Pete mixing in his typical but spare rhythm chatter, nicely creating a sense of call-and-response with his vocal lines. Underscoring this vibe is a country and western windup for the twangy resolution of the song, echoed a couple years later in "Squeeze Box."

Lyrically, Pete puts Jimmy in an introspective place, perhaps walking down the cobblestones wondering why he can't project past a Ticket or a Number—he nakedly calls himself a loser in the song—into that visceral world of Face-dom. As Pete puts it, despite the loneliness on this autumn day, Jimmy's teenage charge lights up some modicum of optimism that, in fact, deep down he is "one" of the elite. Even so, while he's waiting for inspiration, he's at least roughly part of a Mod crowd, if not exactly a shining exemplar. But then Jimmy snuffs his own glow of confidence, lamenting that he can't get the clothes to fit right, his fingers are clumsy, and his voice is too loud, all signs of a lingering struggle with puberty.

Still, through the happy music enveloping Jimmy's words, Pete seems to be telling him that maybe with a little work, or through letting time do its maturing magic, he can be "one," or at least one enough to accomplish the modest goal of fitting in more substantially. Reflecting on the song, Pete calls "I'm One" a favorite and a favorite to play live. But he seems conflicted on how autobiographical it is, on the one hand identifying with being awkward and shy as a teenager but on the other saying that he had been too old to be a proper Mod.

THE DIRTY JOBS

"The Dirty Jobs" was one of Pete's early songs, with his (slightly slower) all-instruments demo having been put to tape on July 25, 1972. For this reason, it precedes the clear plot and plan for *Quadrophenia* and is thus more universal and less linked to Jimmy's Mod life. In the end, Pete imagines Jimmy in actual conversation with these menial workers, one who "looks after the pigs" and one who "drives the bus," with the latter also bringing up the miners who work the pits, his usual customers. The bus driver looks at Jimmy and tells him he's no different and even looks the same, adding a sort of warning to escape while he can. When Jimmy responds, he qualifies that he's still young and perhaps capable of making use of the advice. There's a loose tie here to the talk of job action in Pete's intro essay, with Jimmy in the first person telling us that his fellow trash collectors had considered going on strike.

Musically, Pete's pop music or at least midrock vibe for the track is prescient of where he'd go on the next four albums with The Who. The brief spot of predrums intro music bears a similarity to the intro music of "Cut My Hair." This brings up the point that some of the criticism sent *Quadrophenia*'s way at the time identified a sameness. To be sure, apart from cases where the band literally revisits themes numerous times, there are sections like this and a handful of harder-rocking bits that remind us of things we've heard earlier.

Back to "The Dirty Jobs," Roger sings wistfully and melodically, breathing extra humanity and aspiration into these characters that keep the city running. John does the same, turning in a complex version of the very hummable octave-jumping pattern Pete plays on his demo. Keith, in his own manner, does this as well, almost playing *for* them, blessing their story with attention to detail, which includes an uncommon amount of bass drum to go with his smashed cymbals. (Of note, from an audio point of view, the drums sound better on the demo.) The overall relaxed speed and simple, descending melody of the song further underscore the idea of the humanity of these workers given that it's more the music of a Sunday, the part of the week where we see what they'd rather be doing with their time.

Prominent is Pete's metronomic fiddle part, taking the place of something he'd often do with sequenced synth, which in turn helps fulfill the role of a normal bassist. But Pete doesn't stop there, adding structure-forming synth lines and only occasional and

← The Forum in Los Angeles,
November 23, 1973 →→

distantly mixed guitar, the highlight being an unexpectedly multitracked countrified passage at the break. Also low in the mix is any of the credited piano playing by Chris Stainton, who is most prominently heard executing the sweeping "fill" that introduces the first verse. Left out of the final version is the demo's squirrely synth effect, which Pete likened to a manual laborer going "ow, ow, ow" in pain.

A minute from the end, dovetailed in over the verse music in instrumental and double-time form, we hear a mob of workers clapping in unison at a protest. As Pete fades The Who out, we hear a bit of a John Philip Sousa march called "The Thunderer," which Ron Nevison had taped surreptitiously at a brass performance in Regent's Park.

HELPLESS DANCER

This track went by the working title of "Russian Dance," due to the fact that it was a piano piece Pete had written back in the *Tommy* days inspired by Slavic folk dance. It's the closest thing to opera on the album, with Roger first singing a pomp and circus pants vocal line over naked piano notes, while for the second version, he's joined by Pete with panoramic multi-tracked flamenco guitar.

Lyrically, Pete saw this as part of a set with "The Dirty Jobs," that song's menial workers now more vociferously and eloquently complaining about their meaningless existence within the capitalism machine. Outside the grind of the job is nothing but hunger, homelessness, dashed hopes, beatings, and bombings. But even if it sounds like a screed coming from the workers themselves, Pete has also framed it as Jimmy describing the lives of these workers, railing at them to wake up and break free.

↑ Jimmy on his flash scooter

↑ English session musician, keyboard player, and songwriter Chris Stainton, London, January 1972

↗ Roger, Amsterdam, Netherlands, 1972

If the tales sound like a rant from the middle of a rabid crowd during the Russian Revolution, the music sounds older than that, taking us back to feudal times with the relentless piano stabs but also the lonely flugelhorn line announcing something imminent and not good. Pete has mused that the connection with old music is a suggestion that this is how life has always been back through the generations.

After a long, pregnant pause filled with more ominous music, Roger shouts, "You stop dancing," representing the idea that it's all over once you realize that using the working class as machines is all part of the grand plan of the elites. The title "Helpless Dancer" comes from this idea, a phrase that doesn't figure in the lyrics and frankly sounds a little off, as does the identification of this song as Roger's theme. Pete deemed it as such due to the anger of the lyric and attendant vocal lining up well with Roger and his tendency to solve problems with his fists. Finally, after the song dissolves, we get a snippet of "The Kids Are Alright" being played in a hot and sweaty club, suggesting that at least for now, the kids, including Jimmy, still have dancing, unlike their parents. Then The Who classic fades and we get a haunting and echoey "Is it me? For a moment," which serves as a taunt to the young that the good times surely won't last.

IS IT IN MY HEAD?

This next track came even earlier than "The Dirty Jobs" with Pete penning the song in early 1972 (along with "Love, Reign o'er Me") to break in the new grand piano he'd acquired to replace his upright. Given that there was no *Quadrophenia* yet, the lyric is ill-fitting, sounding partly like Jimmy but also like one of the more thoughtful manual laborers of the previous two songs, or like Pete himself, with Pete admitting that it is a bit autobiographical. The passage that sounds most like Jimmy is the one in which we see the awkward kid with an empty head asking for directions with the words coming out all wrong—again, a mix of puberty and pills.

Along with "Love, Reign o'er Me," this song was recorded at Olympic Studios with the great Glyn Johns credited as engineer and associate producer. Pete pegs the date for his home demo of the track as April 30, 1972, with the full-band execution of the song

↓ Pete plays his old upright piano at his Twickenham home, 1969.

taking place later that summer. The prime motivation at the time was to create music "with more air," to paint a sound picture that would be grand like his new piano. Pete pushed Johns to join him in the quest.

Like so many other *Quadrophenia* songs, the final version of this one is significantly similar to the demo. Then again, all it takes is to put John on bass and Keith on drums to have a transformation. Plus Roger sings instead of Pete, with the added feature of John joining him on the choruses, the only place John sings on the album. Once more, the general structure is of a soft rock song played by a full band with bluster, and the full band this time includes an enthusiastic Pete, who gives us lots of rock guitar and vigorously strummed acoustic, along with additional sighing cross-hatches of sliding and slippery country twang.

I'VE HAD ENOUGH

Closing side two of the original vinyl album is "I've Had Enough," a strident rocker kicked off by Keith. As with "The Dirty Jobs" and "Helpless Dancer," this one finds Jimmy interfacing with an older generation, a denizen of which spits the first two verses, telling Jimmy he's been screwing up. It's sensible that Pete collars Roger for the job, who injects just the perfect amount of vocal fry. But Pete does an amusing job on his demo as well, getting into character, singing angrily, a bit like a Gestapo officer.

The threatening music is shunted aside, after which Jimmy breaks in over a bright and cheery Who jam, telling the old man about how his suit, his GS scooter, his haircut, and finally the overcoat against the weather will soon have him looking and feeling sharp. Notably Pete, the younger-sounding voice of the dynamic Who duo of lead vocalists, takes over for this section, creating a more pronounced partition between characters.

But then suddenly we're into the ominous "Love, Reign o'er Me" theme, followed by the even more uneasy "I've had enough" section, which sounds like a mix of a prayer and suicide note, set to folk music that Pete likened to a bit of a piss-take on The Kingston Trio's "Hang Down Your Head Tom Dooley." In fact, he plays banjo here, which in the end is mixed much further back compared with its presentation on his December 17, 1972, demo of the song.

As the song winds down, there are two more verses about the reality of adult life, followed by another run of the Jimmy-as-Mod chorus and the "Love, Reign o'er Me" pairing. The final list of "I've had enoughs" is markedly different from the first one. Whereas the first time around it sounds like the lament of an old dockworker at the end of his usefulness, now it's Jimmy, and he's thinking about giving up the Mod life and, most heartbreaking, giving up "trying to love." An anguished scream from Roger is followed by ambiguous crash sounds (actually a train screeching against the rails), and the longest, most ambitious, and most prog-minded song on the album is over, emotions of the listener flummoxed and concern for Jimmy growing.

↑ Is Jimmy thinking of leaving the Mods, or are there other regrets in his rearview mirror?

←← "I've Had Enough" is ushered in by a typical yet succinct Keith flourish.

R oger Harry Daltrey was born in East Acton in the west of London on March 1, 1944. Along with Pete and John, he attended Acton County Grammar School, where he proved to be whip-smart, excelling at his studies until he was unceremoniously expelled for smoking (the occasion was later immortalized in the title of Roger's 2018 autobiography, *Thanks a Lot Mr. Kibblewhite*).

At thirteen, Roger had built his own guitar, fashioned out of a chunk of wood to look like a Stratocaster, and in 1959 he was gifted an Epiphone by his father, an insurance clerk who had made it out of World War II after being enlisted near the end of hostilities. This was Roger's instrument of choice in The Detours, which he led heavy-handedly, a punch to the face usually resolving any disputes. The Detours, of course, evolved into The Who, and the power dynamic shifted; Pete did the lion's share of writing and took over on guitar as well, leaving Roger as front man with the majority of the lead vocals. Before the age of ubiquitous information, it looked to many like Roger led the band, and in the realm of decision-making, especially on business matters, he indeed was more than equal to Pete throughout The Who's frantic life cycle.

A week after the band issued its seventh album, *The Who by Numbers*, *Lisztomania*, directed by Ken Russell and starring Roger, was released. This followed the cinematic rendition of *Tommy*, also directed by Russell and starring Roger, issued only six months earlier. Further creating a life outside the fold, Roger also had to his name two solo albums, *Daltrey* (1973) and *Ride a Rocking Horse* (1975), sent to the shops in the space between the two flash and surreal films. Roger, with his trademark long, curly blond hair and square jaw, was becoming a brand and industry unto himself, even if across the brunt of the solo recording career to come, he'd curious stay mostly away from songwriting. This would be the case for moderately successful records like *One of the Boys* from 1977 and *Under a Raging Moon* from 1985, although on the latter, he figures in

four of the credits, with the first single from the album, "After the Fire," written by Pete.

Roger has eight solo albums (depending on how you count) as of 2018, but outside of The Who, his main claim to career and creative fame is as a film and TV actor. Highlights here include *McVicar* (plus the soundtrack album), *The Beggar's Opera*, *The Comedy of Errors*, *Pop Pirates*, *How to Be Cool*, *Mack the Knife*, *Buddy's Song*, *Lightning Jack*, and *Like It Is*, comprising a variety of formats, from episodic TV and TV movies to starring roles and cameos in cinematic productions as well as a healthy dose of musicals. But it's *Tommy* for which he'd garner the most accolades, including a Golden Globe nomination for Best Acting Debut in a Motion Picture.

Elsewhere on his own, Roger appeared at 1992's Freddie Mercury Tribute Concert, singing muscular Queen anthem "I Want It All." For his fiftieth birthday in 1994, he did a couple of solo shows at Carnegie Hall, which prompted a solo U.S. tour. Simon Townshend and John Entwistle were part of the band, the Ox splitting bass duties with Phil Spalding. Roger was back with the *Use It or Lose It* solo tour in late 2009, joined once again by Simon. As recently as 2018, Roger has issued new music, in the form of solo album *As Long as I Have You*, mostly covers but notable in that Pete plays guitar on seven of the album's eleven tracks.

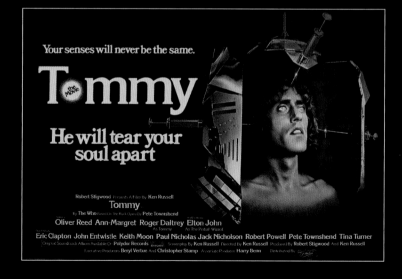

↗ Roger with his Volvo P1800 Coupe at the Duke of York's HQ in Chelsea, London, on November 12, 1966. The Who were making a short live film for German television.

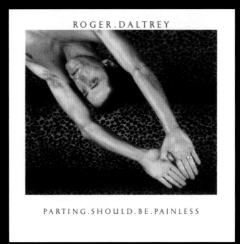

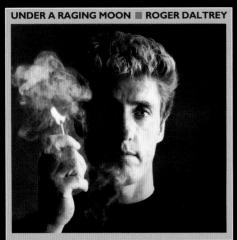

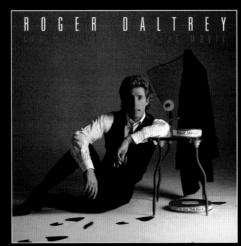

Outside of music, Roger has been the driving force behind The Who's contribution to the Teenage Cancer Trust concert series, taking the band there but also performing as a solo act. He's also been involved with numerous other charitable events, most of them on the medical side of the ledger. Roger has also been politically outspoken for years. Across the suite of issues he's never been afraid to speak upon, he essentially started left and now leans right. Back home, after a rocky rock 'n' roll romantic start to life, Roger married Heather Taylor in 1971, his second and last marriage, producing two daughters and a son. This makes for eight children from various relationships, along with fifteen grandchildren.

All the while, Roger has been the ready, steady other half to Pete as the critical original part of the evolving Who to this day, ever since the band became sporadic after 1982's *It's Hard* album. It goes without saying, but given the passing of Keith and John, there's no question of there still being a Who without Roger Daltrey.

(5)

"Let me flow into the ocean"

← Keith and Roger at the Fête de l'Humanité
music festival, Paris, September 9, 1972.

[SIDE THREE]

87

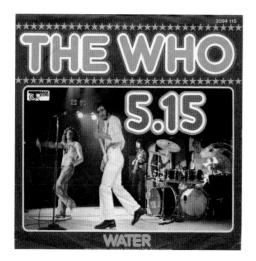

5:15

On September 23, 1973, The Who released what was to be the only U.K. single from the imminent *Quadrophenia* album. The commercial launch of "5:15" (sometimes presented as "5.15" and backed with the non-LP "Water") was followed by a notorious performance of the track on the five-hundredth episode of *Top of the Pops* on October 4, also before the full album hit the shops. Taped for the influential TV show the day before, the guys were in a surly mood, expecting to mime the track and then told they'd have to do a live version as well to be used as backing due to a recent Musicians' Union ruling. The final version was a muddle: a live intro (Pete bums some notes), a live vocal from Roger, and the rest the album track. The band was supposed to use the recorded version from the day before, but that never happened.

Expressing his disdain, at the end of the song, Pete kicks over Keith's drums and then breaks the neck off his valuable go-to studio Chet Atkins Gretsch, which he fortunately was able to repair and still owns to this day. Keith joins in the mayhem, and it instantly becomes obvious that the band has been miming to a tape. Wigs from the prop department are thrown about the stage, and Pete gives the finger to show producer Robin Nash. (The offensive bits were cut from the airing but emerged later during the closing credits of Who documentary *The Kids Are Alright*.) With Pete flipping off Nash and Keith acting up in the green room, the BBC gave The Who a lifetime ban by the BBC, though it was soon smoothed over by a letter of apology sent to the BBC.

"5:15" was issued as a single all over the world (usually with a picture sleeve), but not in North America or Japan, and it reached #20 on the U.K. charts. The United States eventually saw a version of it in 1979 as a single from the *Quadrophenia* film soundtrack album, where it was issued as a picture sleeve backed with "I'm One."

A sort of boogie rocker and the first song on side three of the album, "5:15" was not demoed by Pete, and the band worked it up in the studio. Pete says he wrote the song "in Oxford Street and Carnaby Street while killing time between appointments." The song kicks off with train station sounds captured at Waterloo Station, which also yielded the whistle sounds used just before the band clangs in. Pete had to pay the engineer £5 to blow the whistle so he could capture it on tape, and for his troubles, it's not even heard on all mixes of the song. This represents Jimmy getting on a train back to Brighton, on which he relives good memories, including the clash between the Mods and the Rockers.

↑ The Who perform on *Top of the Pops*, 1973.

← In the commuter train scene from the 1979 film, Jimmy sees his future and he doesn't like it.

←← An elevated view of London's Waterloo Station shows crowds of people leaving trains on platforms 1 and 2.

Getting on, he's in a dark mood, having slept outside in the rain fuming over his girlfriend taking up with his best friend, Dave. This is the same "bird" he had on the beach last time in Brighton. He's also just smashed his scooter, so, armed with two hundred leapers, he takes a handful of them and gets on the train—after talking himself out of jumping in front of it.

The melancholy intro music represents a reprise of the same "Why should I care?" refrain that introduced "Cut My Hair" on side one. This leads into Jimmy ruminating and reminiscing, presumably on the train as pictured in the original booklet. He sits slouched between two businessmen in bowler hats, both engrossed in the daily news and paying no mind to Jimmy. His thoughts kick off with the image—as Pete has confirmed concerning the lyric—of theater ushers spraying cologne on the seats after girls had wet themselves screaming as they watched some pop band up onstage. This tale usually involves The Beatles, but the suggestion here is Jimmy's connection with The Who, going right to the heart of his inner turmoil over whether the band members are heroes worthy of such mania.

Then he pictures in his mind the lead-up to the storied brawl, with Pete offering a bevy of dualities and oxymorons. Unspoken is the face-off between the Mods and the Rockers, but right in the lyrics we get "magically bored," "free frustration," "quiet storm water," "uppers and downers," and "inside outside." In the third verse, where Jimmy derides preoccupation with fashion, there's "greyly outrageous," "tightly undone," and "sadly ecstatic." Most of these phrases are delivered as part of a phrasing pattern that sounds like call and response, underscoring the flummoxed state of Jimmy's left and right brains as good memories spoil.

At the musical end, this is another one somewhat marred by the addition of a horn arrangement, which competes not only with the band rocking nicely but also with the barroom piano parts provided by Chris Stainton and Pete's ample "train song" guitar soloing. For brass, John recorded two trombones, two euphoniums, and four trumpets. At the vocal end, it's Pete sensitively and suitably asking, "Why should I care?" while Roger does the blustery verses, again, in dialogue with a multitracked, casually harmonized gang vocal.

SEA AND SAND

Next, "Sea and Sand" finds The Who back in moderate opera or progressive rock mode, more "bitty," in other words, stitching together parts. The song also uses the device of bringing back earlier themes, namely the happy Mod part from "I've Had Enough," as well as cinematic effects, with the surf and seagulls at the start. There's something elevated and pure of performance here, even sloppier, benefiting from the lack of anything outside of guitar, bass, drums, and vocals, which are a mix of Roger and Pete. Most boisterous are Keith, cymbal bashing and driving the beat, and Pete, who weaves clean and clear acoustic guitars into the song as well as another signature flitting, darting, and departing guitar solo, or more accurately, two tracks of rhythm, panned hard left and hard right, which each cross into solo status at will. Indeed it's Pete left, Pete right, and Keith—and not really John, who is recorded very fat and thus sounds like a bass player doing bass—in battle for the cacophonous closing jam. During this passage, we're back to Pete on vocals, who sings over and over like a mantra, "I'm the face if you want it," a quote from "I'm the Face," the B side to "Zoot Suit," the band's first single recorded as The High Numbers.

Lyrically, Jimmy's now back on the beach in Brighton, telling us he's been kicked out of the house by his drunk parents. He reminisces (not without disdain) about getting it on with his ex-girlfriend on the beach. This passage is sung by Roger over the full band but in wistful ballad mode with Pete on acoustic. But then there's the return to the Mod checklist of "I've Had Enough," followed by a more tender memory, seeing this girl across the dance floor for the first time. This is followed by another run at the "I've Had Enough" part but with new lyrics, where an angry Jimmy, now played by Pete, is incensed that the other Tickets are able to pull off a better Mod look than he does despite spending less on it, an actual point of contention among Mods in the waning days of the movement, when the kit became mainstream and somewhat mass-produced.

Again strengthening the integrity of the song as part of a concept album, we see a return to a musical theme not heard since the beginning of the song, over which Jimmy is deep into his reflection at the passage of time, comparing his choices then, now, and in the future.

DROWNED

This song is another poppy and melodic track that is nonetheless full band and up-tempo. Prominent is a babbling brook of a piano part inspired by Chris Stainton's lick on Joe Cocker's "Hitchcock Railway." On the joyous, percussion-laden demo, Pete played acoustic guitar, but he had Stainton play it on piano for the album version. In addition, Pete, using Keith's full kit at home at this time, gives the song an odd beat, putting the snare on two and the "and" on four. He also includes an uncharacteristically fuzzy lead guitar solo.

Pete wrote the song in tribute to his spiritual master Meher Baba way back in 1970, recording it in March of that year, in part to test out his new 3M M23 eight-track machine and his homemade mixer. Pete actually performed the track in India in January 1972 at

↑ Pete in his Twickenham home studio, 1970

←← Selling *Quadrophenia* to America, Los Angeles, November 22, 1973

← The Ox in his home studio in London, 1972, thinking about something "slightly R&B"

Baba's tomb. When Stainton did his bit, a storm was raging outside and a hole had opened up in the roof, flooding the piano booth. Richard Barnes remembers Stainton opening the door to the booth and water rushing out, also remarking that Ron Nevison was in the mobile capturing the take, oblivious to what was going on inside the converted church. Film director Ken Russell was there to witness the deluge. Nevison confirms that he was holed up recording the take, with Stainton in isolation playing live with the band, when out of the Airstream window he saw the emergency lights from the fire truck pulling up to the building to see if everyone was okay.

Outside of the Stainton drama, the song is a groovy Who workout with Roger singing, sent slightly R&B by John's bass line. After a jam, in which Pete plays in a swirl and Stainton duels with Keith (Keith wins), there's a musical passage that is an approximated, cleverly inverted reprise of the brass section bit from "5:15." After another run at a verse, the jam returns, and this time Stainton and Pete turn it up a notch and Keith turns it up two, underscored by Pete and Nevison putting him prominent in the mix.

Knowing the story of the song's birthing, Pete's lyric is pure and pleasant mystical oneness, with the protagonist as a drop of water and God as the ocean. But suddenly we're plunged into a bracing cold-water scene (see page 39 of the booklet) where Jimmy is half-heartedly trying to drown himself. If we are to marry the two incongruities, Jimmy is half putting a philosophical spin on what he's doing and half hallucinating as he blacks out. As the song fades, we hear the surf and seagulls—and here comes Pete tramping along the beach singing "Sea and Sand."

BELL BOY

The final track on side three of the original vinyl is "Bell Boy," or more formally, "Bell Boy (Keith's Theme)." This aligns with Pete's subplot of making Jimmy's personality a composite of those of the four Who members, which in the early days worked for him. Now, however, Jimmy finds himself flummoxed to the point of traumatized, a situation where he isn't liking what he sees, finding the band, to a man, fraudulent and in the least, not worthy of hero worship. "Bell Boy" fits well with that idea, although it's got little to do with Keith. Jimmy is in Brighton, and he recognizes the face of a Face, one so prominent that he remembers him as "riding in front of a hundred faces," adding that he used to follow this guy back in 1963 (all of this would make him the Ace Face). Jimmy's horrified to find out that this guy is now a lowly bellhop who wears a monkey suit (he's not dressed for work in the encounter), "running at someone's heel," with Keith bringing the character to roughshod life with his Uncle Ernie routine from *Tommy*.

There's a nice meeting of the minds where Jimmy's opening reflection about the beach is later seconded by the ex-Face, who says that sometimes he even sleeps on the beach and then goes straight to work at the hotel. This is the same hotel that Ace vandalized during the riot, smashing in the plate glass door. Jimmy tells us in the intro essay that even while kicking in the door with a sawed-off shotgun stuffed in his coat, Ace still managed to look like "Fred Astaire reborn." Then the Face, noting the deadness of Jimmy's eyes, gives him some advice, but the punch line is ambiguous. He intimates that the secret to his true persona is carried "behind this little badge," which can mean that it's a couple inches behind, in his heart, representing authenticity, or that it's in fact part and parcel of the badge, meaning that his work is the only identity he now has.

At the music end, there's a fresh arrangement different from anything we've heard recently, featuring the whole band and Pete on acoustic guitar and synthesizer. Keith is playing a tight, doubled-up beat with the snare on every beat. Things slow down for Keith's more pastoral singing bits, where it's not all Uncle Ernie—perhaps some of it is Ray Davies. Once the music picks up, Pete adds a new high-pitched and prominent synth part. Also distinctive is Pete's use of some of the most powerful power chords on the album, not to mention Keith's big gong washes!

Pete seems ambivalent about Keith's hammy portrayal of the Face, amused that it injected an unexpected and unplanned component to what Pete pictured but also not sure about infusing humor into the equation. It's been a repeated tradition on past Who records, but it's an ill fit here, especially three-quarters of the way through a double album. On his poppy, intimate yet quite elaborate demo—think 10cc—Pete sings all the parts, and, as he's ruminated in later liner notes about the record, he wonders if there'd be more anger in the track if he'd collared Roger to sing it. Indeed, the contrast would have been palpable back on July 31, 1973—both Keith's "Bell Boy" vocal and Roger's "I've Had Enough" vocal were recorded that day. As Pete recalls, Keith's singing had the guys in tears with laughter while, as Pete phrased it, Roger's singing "scared the hell out of us."

↑ Sting from The Police, on the job as a bellboy in the 1979 film

→→ Keith looks on with disdain as the "Ace Face" of the Mods is forced to work as a bellboy. No amount of gong added to his signature song of the same name would drown out his disgust at the situation.

Keith was Moon the Loon from the outset. Born Keith John Moon on August 23, 1946, in North London, Keith was the onboard entertainment in school until he escaped at age fourteen. He joined the cadets on bugle but found the instrument too difficult, and he turned to drums, which sounded like explosions, his other love—first through home science kits and later through cherry bombs. Keith managed to train in radio repair at Harrow Technical College—forget about grammar school, with one teacher deeming him "retarded artistically. Idiotic in other respects"—which allowed him to afford his first drum kit.

Keith developed his distinct style from a base in jazz and R&B, although lessons with the notoriously hard-hitting Carlo Little from Screaming Lord Sutch & the Savages (plus The Rolling Stones, in the early days) also helped. Previously with The Escorts and then The Beachcombers, Keith joined The Who in April 1964. He had already developed his uncommon technique, characterized by judicious use of toms and cymbals played almost symphonically like classical percussion instruments, rather than to keep time. John contributed one of the more insightful things about Keith, saying that Keith had two sets of toms because he moved his arms forward like a skier versus left to right like a normal person.

Keith was also an early pioneer of double bass drums, although actually playing them was more of an afterthought for him. Adjacent to that, Keith was a pioneer of big drum kits.

People would also say that Keith played "lead drums"—what he did defined many Who songs structurally as much as what anybody else did, besides Roger. Roger anchored the song, a job usually held by the bass player, while Keith, John, and Pete dovetailed in and out of their expected rock 'n' roll duties. John spent 75 percent of the time extrapolating on the bass part and only 25 percent of the time playing it. Pete did roughly the same thing with respect to guitar parts, specializing in licks rather than riffs or chord sequences. The result was that three-quarters of what The Who did was unexpected, despite fairly conventional songwriting from Pete to get the ball rolling.

Unfortunately, Keith quickly got hooked on pills, brandy, champagne, and his own legend, figuring his job while in the band and also when on leave was to make everybody laugh, more than it was to be a drummer. Up until *Quadrophenia*, Pete was already trying to save Keith through proper employment, first with the studio work and touring, where, ironically, Keith could get into less trouble, or at least less of a mental funk, even though he still went mental.

Outside of The Who, Keith tried his hand at radio as well as film, playing bit parts in *200 Motels*, *That'll Be the Day*, *Stardust*, *Sextette*, and Ken Russell's *Tommy*, in which he played Uncle Ernie. Always up for a party, he stumbled into various percussion and backing vocal situations live and on record with assorted famous friends. He was also good for one lark of a solo album, *Two Sides of the Moon*, considered one of the worst records of all time and certainly one of the worst very expensive albums of all time. It took about fifty people, many of them quite distinguished musicians, to make the album—ten short songs, all covers, with Keith singing—and it was savaged by the critics.

But there were worse travesties. Already bleeding The Who coffers through his destruction of hotel rooms—estimated at half a million dollars over the course of less than a decade—on November 20, 1973, at the Cow Palace in San Francisco, Keith embarrassed the band most publicly by passing out at his kit, making way for concertgoer Scot Halpin to be plucked from the crowd and finish the set.

It might be proposed that Keith's move to Los Angeles sealed his fate. There he became part of the infamous Hollywood Vampires, drinking and drugging through the night with Harry Nilsson, Alice Cooper, Ringo Starr, Micky Dolenz, and

↙ Keith pictured in the *Daily Mirror* studios in 1977, dressed in court jester costume and makeup to entertain the children of the Barnardo Day Centre at Forest Gate, East London

← Lord Moon of Shepperton, 1977

↙ Keith attends the premiere of *The Buddy Holly Story* in the West End with fiancée Annette Walter-Lax as guests of Paul and Linda McCartney, September 6, 1978. After dining with Paul and Linda at Peppermint Park in Covent Garden, Keith and Annette returned to their flat where he was found dead early the next morning after overdosing on thirty-two tablets of clomethiazole, prescribed to alleviate his alcohol-withdrawal symptoms.

occasionally John Lennon and Bernie Taupin. Keith was markedly damaged by the time of his last tour leg with The Who in 1976 in support of *The Who by Numbers*, and he was even worse during the studio sessions for *Who Are You*, frustrated and his confidence shattered.

Before the end, there would be two isolated shows, both disastrous. First came the band's lone 1977 date, December 15, at the Gaumont State Cinema in Kilburn, North London, for the filming of *The Kids Are Alright*. This was followed by Keith's last show ever, May 25, 1978, at Shepperton Studios, also for the film. Keith was overweight, very nervous, and at his very least capable. Outside these two specialty shows—ragged jams at which Pete, John, and Roger (not to mention Keith) could see the writing on the wall—the band's last proper gig as part of a tour was a stop at Maple Leaf Gardens in Toronto, way back on October 21, 1976.

Threatened with firing in 1976 and again in 1978 after the recording of *Who Are You*, Keith was in such a state that the band couldn't tour. He had moved back to Britain and was living in the London flat where Cass Elliot from The Mamas and the Papas had died. At this point he was living with Swedish model Annette Walter-Lax, and on September 6, 1978, the two were invited at the behest of Paul and Linda McCartney to a filming of *The Buddy Holly Story*. In an attempt to get sober, Keith was prescribed a drug called Heminevrin to curb his craving for alcohol, and the party went off without incident. Back home, Keith went to bed and never woke up. An autopsy determined that Keith had twenty-six Heminevrin in his system; he was told never to take more than three a day. Keith's nine lives were up at thirty-two, after eight records with The Who. (John Bonham died at the same age, suffering a somewhat similar demise two years later after eight records with Led Zeppelin.)

6 "Oh God, I need a drink of cool, cool, cool rain"

← John performs with his Gibson/Fender hybrid "Fenderbird" bass on the *Popgala* TV show, The Hague, Netherlands, March 10, 1973.

[SIDE FOUR]

DOCTOR JIMMY

The last side of *Quadrophenia* sounds like one big final chord, a windup that takes place over the course of three songs and twenty-one minutes. But "Doctor Jimmy"—formally "Doctor Jimmy (Including John's Theme Is It Me?)"—starts purposefully enough. Waves, howling wind, and sirens give way to dramatic, regal synths that collapse into the first verse, with Roger singing powerfully over a propulsive pop backing track featuring uncommonly sparse playing from the rhythm section. Most notable is Pete's vigorous violin playing, carried over from the demo. Incidentally, Pete was frustrated that he had to suspend work on his demos after recording this song on July 27, 1972, due to the band being booked on a "rather pointless" European tour in August and September. And then he had to work on the orchestral version of *Tommy* for a spell, as well as serve in a production role for Eric Clapton, whom Pete had also been nursing through a heroin addiction.

Back to the finished track, once we get to the elaborate prechorus and chorus configuration, we hear John's nicely integrated horn arrangements, recorded smartly and working well due to the percussive pomp of the parts. After another verse, prechorus, and chorus, we're into an orchestral and atmospheric transition that leads into the "Is it me, for a moment?" theme, followed by more orchestral music—this time with Roger singing. Two runs of this are followed by a modulation in key and then another verse. Then we hear a series of prechoruses but no chorus. Instead, there's a drop out to a sort of folky classical bit, followed by entirely new driving instrumental music. Finally, there's another chorus, followed by more orchestral messing about, marbled once again with the "Is it me, for a moment?" theme. One can picture Pete biding his time, trying to figure out how to end the story. This fades into a morass of classical piano jangling and a hint of the "Love, Reign o'er Me" theme.

→ Rarin' for a fight (or a back-alley fumble), *Quadrophenia*, 1979

→→ Pete and Eric Clapton perform at the Rainbow Theatre, Finsbury Park, London, January 13, 1973.

As for the lyric, we find Jimmy talking about the mean side that comes out "when I drink my gin," a classic Dr. Jekyll and Mr. Hyde story, only this time it's Dr. Jimmy and Mr. Jim. Curiously, he qualifies that "you don't notice him" when he's "pilled." But get the drink in him and he's rarin' for a fight, all the while more worried about his clothes than a bloody nose. The other time gin is referenced is in Pete's intro essay, where Jimmy takes a slug of Gilbey's gin halfway to the rocks after nicking the boat. We learn that generally Jimmy's not a boozer and that he and alcohol don't get along.

He's also a predator; Pete now cringes that he used the line "Who is she? I'll rape it" (along with "lesbians and queers" and "blacks" in "Helpless Dancer," while we're at it). This one's also got "You say she's a virgin/I'm gonna be the first in." The idea, of course, is that Jimmy's out of control and out of touch with empathy. Pete assures us through other lyrics that Jimmy essentially has empathy at his core, and the recurring "Is it me, for a moment?" passages suggest that deep down he is troubled by this side of him, with the end reflections sounding fatalistic. In fact, the closing line, where he wonders if something stronger could hold him down, rides the razor's edge between medicine and willful overdose.

To what extent does it make sense to call this John's theme? More so than Roger's "Helpless Dancer" and Keith's "Bell Boy," and somewhat on par with Pete's "Love, Reign o'er Me." John had a dark side and was a profligate hell-raiser with a big ego, consuming booze, cocaine, and women at a rate equal to that of Keith, the difference being that his ticket to death by misadventure, eventually punched, was good for longer.

THE ROCK

Concerning "The Rock," Pete writes in the original booklet that "the four themes are heard again, then they all combine, four into one." However, Pete didn't get to take the idea to its planned conclusion. He had originally wanted each of the four themes to be heard in separate quadraphonic channels before coming together for an overlapped cacophony in mono straight down the middle, after which they were to disperse again into each of their proscribed corners. Pete recorded his demo for the song using an elaborate system of bouncing tracks from March 25 through May 1, 1973.

As it stands, "The Rock" is a labyrinth and more so as part of a set with "Quadrophenia" and the many places where Pete inserted unnamed instrumentals into erstwhile regular songs. Any new music we hear within the song isn't particularly exciting. What we get are fresh and ambitious expositions of earlier music, beginning with "Bell Boy," followed by "Is It Me?" and then "Helpless Dancer," linked by an atmospheric sound collage that Pete likens to waves crashing up on Jimmy's rocks. Pete singles out Keith's drumming in particular—indeed, across the whole album, Keith's predilection for doing single stroke rolls on cymbals with the shaft of his sticks (or beaters) becomes a coincidental and useful tool to evoke surf ebbing and flowing.

After a strident, symphonic take on the "Helpless Dancer" intro, we lurch into a comedic arrangement, where Pete interprets Roger's vocal with staccato single notes on guitar, followed by a modulation in key and a rise in intensity and eventually a harmonized passage. Then we're into the "Love, Reign o'er Me" theme, in which Pete evokes prime, epic, and electric David Gilmour. There's a dissipation and then even more "Helpless Dancer" with a hint of "Bell Boy" and some talk-box-like synth that edges toward lyrics. We hear thunder and then rain, and it's all over.

There are no lyrics to "The Rock," but Pete—one of the best at extending the stories of his songs by talking about them in interviews or writing about them in essays, books, or liner notes—helpfully explains that Jimmy finds himself soaking wet, sitting out on a

←← Jimmy, on the rocks

rock in the ocean, still on the verge of suicide but then struck with enough of an epiphany to get ashore and muddle on. Pete had planned for the simultaneous playing of all four themes to represent Jimmy's sudden self-awareness, which would be sent further toward a "life flashing before your eyes" moment by the overlay of wave and storm sounds. There's also a nice parallel to be drawn between this wordless song and the fact that on the way to "The Rock," Jimmy experiences a kind of mystical audio drone, his head muddled by the combination of leapers, gin, and the hum of the engine on his stolen boat. He likens it to pianos, heavenly choirs, and orchestras, and as a representation of spiritual clarity, it sobers him up. In any event, Pete intimates that all the emotions Jimmy has gone through in rapid succession over the past few days have created a sort of tempered armor protecting a hard-won inner wisdom that will allow him to live, probably still at sea but also on the baby steps of a mystical path toward being one with the sea.

LOVE, REIGN O'ER ME

Quadrophenia ends with the impossibly epic "Love, Reign o'er Me," designated as Pete's theme in the original booklet. Pete recorded his demo for the song on May 10, 1972, making it an early one and furthermore not a deliberate *Quadrophenia* song. Pete had intended to put "The Rock," which was originally titled "Finale—The Rock," at the end of the album but then switched them around. It was a good move given a sort of aimlessness to "The Rock" and a definite musical and emotional potency to "Love, Reign o'er Me."

The song opens with rain, a very grand piano, and an even grander timpani and gong. Then Roger begins singing over the song's memorable synth loop and surging acoustic guitars. Keith kicks in and we're into the dramatic descending chorus line, Roger roaring louder than any previous place on the album. There's a modulated break, featuring a hectic Keith and more novel synth work from Pete as well as some spare but very musical rhythm playing—this constitutes the only sort of happy or hopeful music in the song. Put another way, if the rest of the song might be framed as hopeful, Pete paints the idea of hope as serious business.

Soon we're back to the signature synth riff, which Pete now solos over. Roger then screams out "Love!" and we're into the dramatic chorus once again with Pete continuing to solo. Roger has remarked that what he did with the song was add a level of anger and frustration "from the street," which is not at all what Pete had intended. Pete needed convincing by Ron Nevison and soon thereafter began to appreciate fully what Roger brought to the track. Things go quiet, and then it's time for the big, noisy windup where everybody goes nuts for nearly a full minute.

"Love, Reign o'er Me" was issued in edited form as the second single from the album in North America (both nonpicture sleeve), backed with "Water." It was also issued in Belgium and the Netherlands, backed with "Is It in My Head?" and again notably not in the U.K. The track rose to an unimpressive #76 on the Billboard Hot 100, not faring much better with Cashbox, reaching #54, or with RPM in Canada, reaching #31. Of all the Who albums from *Tommy* through *Who Are You*, *Quadrophenia*, despite being a double, lives on as the least impressive in terms of smash singles.

Pete wrote the brief lyric as a love song to Welsh singer Shirley Bassey, whom he saw live performing with his dad's band when he was eleven and she was about nineteen. In turn, Pete figured his lyric applied to himself autobiographically as much as it did to love. Coming back around, Jimmy, cleansed by the rain, has an epiphany about love. Pete has also pointed out that Meher Baba said that rain was a blessing from God and thunder was God speaking.

→→ Pete in the throes of "Pete's theme," aka "Love, Reign o'er Me," Los Angeles, 1973

Pete has also said that the song is designated as his own theme because it reflects in his persona the "beggar" and the "hypocrite." He also posits that Jimmy is realizing that the four members of The Who are not to be put on a pedestal. He also says that while on the rock, Jimmy prays. All three of these musings are hard to reconcile with the lyric and sound like Pete adding layers of meaning after the fact, if not serving as tacit admission that he didn't get planned points across.

What's clearer is the relationship to Jimmy's plight. He's out there stranded on the rock, already soaked to the bone from jumping into the water, but now it's raining on him as well, creating a situation where Jimmy just might be in the act of committing suicide by rain. Down the mystical end, love makes it rain, and as suggested by the title, love *is* rain. Notwithstanding the rain/reign homophone, Jimmy is asking for love to reign over him, but very clearly, rain is raining/reigning down on him, and he's freezing cold because of it. (Of note, we learn in Pete's essay that the boat has drifted off, so presumably Jimmy's going to have to swim back!) Augmenting a circuit of equations is the association of rain with tears and lovers' sweat and the idea of the sea kissing the beach. Conversely, the dry and dusty road represents the opposite of love, or time spent "apart alone."

Essentially, Pete marches Roger right to the lip of the stage to spell out the moral of the entire *Quadrophenia* album in terms that couldn't be clearer: "Only love can make it rain." By this he's not talking about Jimmy solving his problems by getting back with his girl but rather that each act of love with a girl, his mates, his parents, or strangers and a life guided by love will inch him toward the mystical oneness represented by millions of raindrops falling and becoming one with the ocean.

↑ Pete wrote the brief lyric of "Love Reign o'er Me" for Welsh singer Shirley Bassey, whom he saw live performing with his dad's band when he was eleven.

↖ Jimmy works out that The Who are not to be put on a pedestal.

↞ London, November 1973. Given Daltrey's inspired performance, "Love Reign o'er Me" became as much about Roger as Pete.

John Alec "the Ox" Entwistle was born on October 9, 1944, in Chiswick, West London. His parents were musical, and while John was still a boy, they divorced, his mother raising him at his grandparents' house. Piano lessons at age seven led to brass instruments—John and school chum Pete Townshend briefly tried their hand at jazz—then guitar and finally bass. He quickly took up rock 'n' roll with local roustabout Roger Daltrey, with whom he featured in his first serious band, The Detours. John then persuaded Roger to take in Pete, and The Who was born.

Within the band, John was considered the best musician, quietly an arranger (mostly of brass) and occasional writer and singer, with his songs leaning oddly dark and comical. In a sense, he provided novelty bonus tracks, set apart due to the fact that he would be inclined to sing his allotted track. In any event, it was never enough. John would often grouse about how much of the songwriting space was taken up by Pete, and spent his life feeling unappreciated, compensating with booze, cocaine, gourmet food, relentless infidelities despite being married since 1967, and an expensive collecting habit (including suits of armor, train sets, taxidermy, basses, and luxury cars, even though he never bothered to learn to drive).

Like Jack Bruce, he wanted to make sure he was the loudest guy onstage, commandeering his famous distorted, treble-heavy bass sound through a bank of Marshalls. Onstage, he displayed an array of techniques, sometimes with a pick and sometimes with his fingers, using tapping and a "typewriter" approach (a sort of all-hands-on-deck expansion of tapping), harmonics, and chords, plus left-hand slides and heavy kerranging plucking, sharpened sometimes by assigning a separate pickup to each string. This he would do while retaining a famously detached stage presence, remaining fairly still, facial expression to the minimum, in comical contrast to the high athleticism of the other three guys. The contrast would be at its highest point during bouts of auto-destruction, as John looked on with a mix of amusement and mock disdain.

In large part exacerbated by John, The Who famously made the Guinness Book of World Records in 1976 for playing the loudest concert in history, achieving 126 decibels. From then on and for years to come, they commanded press inches as the loudest band on the planet. As a result, John wound up with near total hearing loss, but true to his nickname, he kept "quiet" about it versus Pete, who actually did a lot to bring one of rock 'n' roll's dirty secrets to prominence as a problem.

As a result of John's creative frustration in The Who, he was the first to assemble a solo album. *Smash Your Head Against the Wall*, issued in May 1971, was followed quickly by *Whistle Rymes*, *Rigor Mortis Sets In*, and *Mad Dog*. John would achieve his greatest solo success with 1981's *Too Late the Hero*, on which he played bass and sang as part of a trio with Joe Walsh and Joe Vitale. There'd also be an archival album of 1985 and 1986 sessions released as *The Rock* in 1996 and a science-fiction cartoon soundtrack album called *Music from Van-Pires* in 2000.

And John loved to play. He regularly toured with his solo band, had a supergroup in 1990 called The Best, did a stint with Ringo Starr & His All-Starr Band in 1995, and even performed with Alan Parsons's Beatles tribute troupe in A Walk Down Abbey Road. He was also a visual artist and, as Pete found out after his death, a long-time Freemason.

Still, within The Who, he managed to amass a nice clutch of credits, including "Boris the Spider," "Cousin Kevin," "When I Was a Boy," "My Wife," "Success Story," "905," "Trick of the Light," "The Quiet One," and three songs on *It's Hard*, many of which were regularly played live.

At the personal end, it was a life of hell-raising with Keith, multiple marriages and relentless cheating, and aggressive and obsessive spending. As his son, Chris, put it, what money didn't go up his nose was left in "stuff," the various collections filling up his massive fifty-five-room Quarwood mansion. It was crowded with curios at the time of his death, many of which were sold off to pay tax bills.

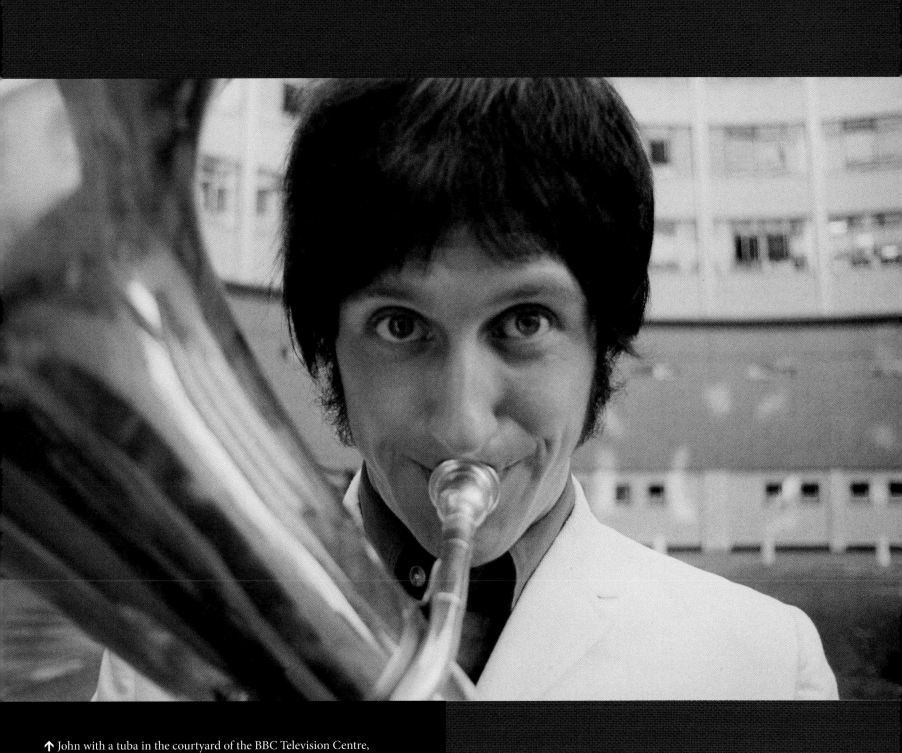

↑ John with a tuba in the courtyard of the BBC Television Centre, London, January 5, 1966. The band was booked to perform two tracks, "Out in the Street" and "It's Not True," on the first episode of the music television show *A Whole Scene Going*.

↑ "I've been a naughty boy." The Ox shows off some of his 120 basses (plus the odd guitar), December 12, 1977.

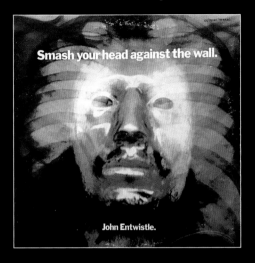

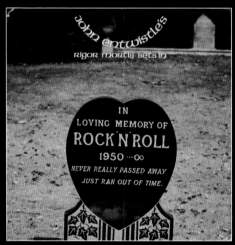

On June 27, 2002, the night before the band's first show of a planned 2002 U.S. tour, John died in his sleep at the Hard Rock Hotel and Casino in Las Vegas. An autopsy discovered that on top of the high blood pressure that ran in the family, one of his arteries was 100 percent blocked and another 75 percent blocked. The Who's 2002 tour was postponed to five days later, and Pete's solo band bassist Pino Palladino took over for the Ox, silenced at fifty-seven years of age.

"You fight computers and receipts"

7

[THE TOUR]

The tour in support of *Quadrophenia* got off to an unceremonious start when Roger punched Pete, cutting the rehearsal time for the new complicated set list in half, from two days to one. In an atmosphere of general stress and exhaustion, not to mention side-taking in the financial battles with Kit Lambert and Chris Stamp, there was the matter of Pete wanting to bring Chris Stainton along on the tour to cover the new album's many piano parts. Roger objected, and the band opted to go with numerous prerecorded passages. The choice caused other issues, mostly with Keith not being able to wrap his head around precise timing, but it was sorted out over time and with practice. The whole thing was a big deal, requiring three trucks carrying twenty tons of equipment and a crew of thirty. The plan for four screens also fell through, and it was always difficult in the smaller venues to find a place to fit the complete quad system.

→→ On home soil celebrating a job well done, October 1973

↓ "Carry this baggage out." Keith in the studio, 1973

The first show revealed these issues, and there was an added complication of Pete's alternate tunings requiring him to change guitars over twenty times. Still, the fans got quadraphonic sound, with John playing a trumpet in "Helpless Dancer." In retrospect, it became a rare set list, for after Stoke-on-Trent, "The Dirty Jobs," "Is It in My Head?," and "I've Had Enough" were dropped from the running order.

At the second show in Wolverhampton, Pete admitted to the crowd that the previous night's show had sounded "bloody horrible." Now, on night two, the guys were going to deliver only "five-eighths" of the new album, said Pete. By press accounts, the band and fans both enjoyed themselves, despite the vocal PA being inadequate, most notably during Keith's "Bell Boy" vocal, which could barely be heard. As for the rest of the set, preceding the abridged *Quadrophenia* were "I Can't Explain," "Summertime Blues," and "My Generation." After *Quadrophenia* came a reprise of "My Generation" along with "Pinball Wizard," "See Me, Feel Me," and "Won't Get Fooled Again." The order shuffled around a bit as the tour marched on. The most notable change was the addition of "My Wife" near the beginning of the later shows.

Night three in Manchester included an encore featuring "Magic Bus" and a cover of Free's "All Right Now." Things came to a head at the first Newcastle show. During "5:15," about thirty-five minutes into the gig, there was a technical breakdown with the backing tapes, manifesting in a delay that the band hobbled through. Pete then attacked road manager Bobby Pridden and dragged him onto center stage, next leaping over to the soundboard, yanking out wires and generally wrecking the prerecorded tape system. Knocking over a few things, he then stalked offstage, with the band later returning for a ten-minute jam version of "Sea and Sand" (some think they heard a bit of "Spoonful" and

↗ Fans are restrained by police on October 22, 1973, while queuing for tickets to upcoming concerts at the Lyceum Ballroom, London. The band would play three nights at the venue, November 11, 12, and 13.

"My Generation") before calling it a disaster of a night. After Pete and Keith went on local TV the next day to explain themselves, there were two more nights to go in Newcastle, followed by three special small-venue shows at the Lyceum in London to close out the wobbly U.K. tour leg.

Over in the United States a week later, the guys first pitched up to the Cow Palace in San Francisco, playing on November 20 with Lynyrd Skynyrd opening in support. They'd almost got to the end of the show, nearly finishing "Won't Get Fooled Again," when Keith passed out and collapsed backward off his drum stool. As Pete remembers it, Keith had taken three elephant tranquilizers (washed down with brandy, his booze of choice), but others say he was offered a drink spiked with PCP.

They somehow revived Keith and, like a Keystone Kops routine, wrestled him back to the kit, limbs flailing. They proceeded to jam a bit of blues and make some noise, Roger playing the harmonica. But then Keith was out again, slumped forward over the kit, and had to be carried out by two roadies. Artimus Pyle, drummer for Lynyrd Skynyrd, was lounging backstage at the time. He was asked to sit in but couldn't muster the courage. Pete then asked the crowd, "Can anybody play the drums?" He asked again, adding, "I mean, somebody good." This is when Scot Halpin, all of nineteen years old, came up and finished the night, performing on "Smokestack Lightning" and "Spoonful," finally struggling through the band's own "Naked Eye," an evolved jam of a song that, granted, wasn't the most intuitive song for a scratch drummer to get right.

Skynyrd, out promoting its very first album, supported the next two nights at the Forum in Los Angeles (the southern rock legends played with The Who on all but one of the next clutch of North American dates, skipping only November 27 at the Omni in Atlanta). Miraculously, Keith was back in business. The first night featured an encore rendition of a song made famous by Marvin Gaye called "Baby Don't You Do It," along

with Pete smashing his guitar. As the American tour progressed, Pete's concern grew over both his and Roger's predilection to explain the *Quadrophenia* plot to U.S. audiences, almost apologetically, surmising that they wouldn't know what a Mod was. This constant qualification led to a sort of piss-taking of their own album, as both became guilty of trying to shorten the preambles, thereby diminishing the impact through an air of dismissiveness.

Seven shows later, The Who was in Montreal. Roger was nursing a cold and having microphone problems to boot. Pete, annoyed at the crowd hootin' and hollerin' during the quiet bits (this is cited as one of the reasons he "invented" the Marshall stack back in 1965!), makes a crack about whether the crowd thought it was at a hockey game. He then skated around the stage using his guitar as a hockey stick.

But there was no smashing. That was reserved for later that night. At the aftershow party put together by the record company at the Hotel Bonaventure, Keith splashed some ketchup on the wall and then decided to frame it with a picture frame after punching out what was in it. Pete cut his hand and smeared blood on the wall, adding to the new work of art. Then a couch and a TV went out the window into the courtyard, and partygoers joined in and destroyed the rest of the room, including a bit of the next one when a heavy marble table was used to smash in an adjoining wall. The cops were called, and everybody at the party—upward of eighteen people—was arrested. They all spent the night in jail, and the guys missed their scheduled flight to Boston. The promoter forked over thousands of dollars to the hotel to make things right. (You can hear all about it on "Cell Number 7" from John's *Mad Dog* album, made a year later after the drywall dust had settled.)

Managing to get to Boston, the same thing that happened at the home of the Canadiens happened at the home of the Bruins—during quiet passages in the studious new songs, the mob called out alternate requests. Pete got ticked off and admonished the crowd.

↑ "Just a warning, the room might need a bit of extra cleaning." John turns in his last hotel key after the U.S. *Quadrophenia* tour. The final show was at the Capital Centre outside of Washington, D.C.

↖ On the plane home from the U.S. *Quadrophenia* tour, December 8, 1973

↑ The L.A. Forum, November 22, 1973, with a complete ticket for the show

There would be no encore, but the next night in Philadelphia there was, an eleven-minute version of "Naked Eye." The U.S. tour finished at the storied Capital Centre on the outskirts of Washington, D.C. The guys then returned to London for a four-night stand at Edmonton Sundown, supported by Babe Ruth. Reflecting a shared and growing animosity toward the recent songs, these shows featured a longer back end of hits, although *Quadrophenia* was still very strongly represented.

Next in February 1974 came six shows in France. The *Quadrophenia* suite was shortened but still formed the bulk of the show. Up into May, concurrent with the filming of the *Tommy* movie and work on the music for the soundtrack album, the band played a smaller venue show of old hits in Oxford, a regular show in Portsmouth, and a big package date at the Charlton Athletic pitch, headlining the Summer of 74 festival over and above Montrose, Maggie Bell, Lindisfarne, Bad Company, Humble Pie, and Lou Reed.

By the band's four-night residency in June 1974 at Madison Square Garden in Manhattan, *Quadrophenia*'s representation had been whittled down to (and not all at each show) "5:15," "Bell Boy," "Doctor Jimmy," "I'm One," and "Drowned," the latter

always a favorite due to its openness to improvisation, in part because it didn't need tapes. Then that was it, eight months elapsed without a particularly large number of performances to show for it.

Away from the double album's tour cycle and into 1976, you'd be lucky to hear two *Quadrophenia* songs in a set. The experience of trying to explain the songs and then play them, sometimes interfaced with technology, turned out to be a chore, exacerbated by the drummer's unpredictable state of mind and subsequent control of his limbs. What's more, as reviews would attest, concertgoers often weren't familiar with the material and may not have had the appetite for the conceptual nature of it or even the very British concept itself. And then they were asked to listen to a bunch of it, one song after another. The hostility of the mob was so bad at the first show in New York that Pete says he had to get roaring drunk just to get through the next three. Pete came home from the tour exhausted and a raging alcoholic. He wrote a long letter to the record company saying he was fed up with everything and everybody and was quitting the band. Fortunately, he never sent it.

↑ Pete succumbs to gravity at the L.A. Forum.

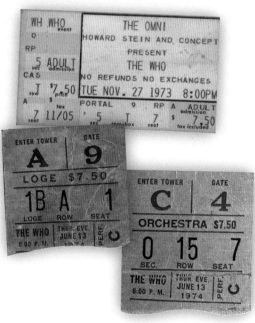

← The L.A. Forum, November 22, 1973

↑ From the second of two shows at the L.A. Forum, November 23, 1973

← Pete directs traffic (not that John is on the move) at one of the band's four Madison Square Garden shows in June 1974.

125

Figuring out a start and stop point for the *Quadrophenia* tour is a snap. The first show, performed two days after the album hit the shops on October 26, 1973, was the band's first concert since March 10 of that year (a short-set festival date at which no *Quadrophenia* songs were played). At the other end, after the Madison Square Garden stand in mid-June 1974, the guys wouldn't play again until October 3, 1975, the same day fans were able to pick up a copy of *The Who by Numbers.*

1973

OCTOBER
28—Trentham Gardens, Stoke-on-Trent, U.K.
29—Civic Hall, Wolverhampton, U.K.

NOVEMBER
1—Kings Hall at Belle Vue, Manchester, U.K.
2—Kings Hall at Belle Vue, Manchester, U.K.
5—Odeon Cinema, Newcastle, U.K.
6—Odeon Cinema, Newcastle, U.K.
7—Odeon Cinema, Newcastle, U.K.
11—Lyceum Ballroom, London, U.K.
12—Lyceum Ballroom, London, U.K.
13—Lyceum Ballroom, London, U.K.
20—Cow Palace, San Francisco, CA, U.S.A.
22—The Forum, Inglewood, CA, U.S.A.
23—The Forum, Inglewood, CA, U.S.A.
25—Convention Center, Dallas, TX, U.S.A.
27—The Omni, Atlanta, GA, U.S.A.
28—St. Louis Arena, St. Louis, MO, U.S.A.
29—International Amphitheatre, Chicago, IL, U.S.A.
30—Cobo Hall, Detroit, MI, U.S.A.

DECEMBER
2—Montreal Forum, Montreal, QC, Canada
3—Boston Garden, Boston, MA, U.S.A.
4—The Spectrum, Philadelphia, PA, U.S.A.
6—Capital Centre, Landover, MD, U.S.A.
18—Edmonton Sundown, London, U.K.
19—Edmonton Sundown, London, U.K.
22—Edmonton Sundown, London, U.K.
23—Edmonton Sundown, London, U.K.

1974

FEBRUARY
9—Palais des Grottes, Cambrai, France
10—Parc des Expositions, Paris, France
15—Les Arènes, Poitiers, France
17—Le Stadium Municipal, Toulouse, France
22—Parc des Expositions, Nancy, France
24—Palais des Sports, Lyon, France

MAY
6—New Theatre, Oxford, U.K.
18—Charlton Athletic Football Club, London, U.K.
22—The Guildhall, Portsmouth, U.K.

JUNE
10—Madison Square Garden, New York, NY, U.S.A.
11—Madison Square Garden, New York, NY, U.S.A.
13—Madison Square Garden, New York, NY, U.S.A.
14—Madison Square Garden, New York, NY, U.S.A.

THE WHO

COW PALACE · NOV 20

Singer

©1973 BILL GRAHAM • TEA LAUTREC LITHO • SAN FRANCISCO

Two Hundred Fifty Thousand People, Eleven Cities In Eighteen Days. Thank You.

Quadrophenia. Two Record Set. Forty-eight Page Booklet. MCA2-10004.
MCA Records. Track Record.

BILL GRAHAM PRESENTS

FALLOUT SHELTER
The Who
North American Tour
1973

Tuesday November 20th
8 p.m.
Cow Palace

Tickets $6.50 (PLUS 50¢ SERVICE CHARGE) ON SALE THURSDAY, NOVEMBER 1
MAXIMUM TWO TICKETS PER PERSON. Available ONLY at TICKETRON
Outlet Listed Below

DISCOUNT RECORD STORES IN: Berkeley and Reno. MONTGOMERY WARD STORES IN: Corte
Madera, Daly City, Fremont, Oakland, Pleasant Hill, Richmond, San Jose and San Leandro.
EMPORIUM STORES IN: Mt. View, Palo Alto, San Francisco (Downtown & Stonestown), San
Jose, San Mateo, San Rafael, Santa Clara and Santa Rosa. THE BOOKMARK IN: Fremont, NEIL
THRAMES IN: Oakland. DOWNTOWN BOX OFFICE IN: Sacramento. COW PALACE IN: San
Francisco. SAN JOSE BOX OFFICE, Town & Country Village, San Jose, TRESIDDER TICKET
OFFICE, Stanford Campus.

QUADROPHENIA QUADROPHENIA

THE
WHO

I've had members of Black Sabbath and the Alice Cooper group tell me about this, and it's definitely part of *Quadrophenia* lore as well: The Who's new album ran into the great PVC (polyvinylchloride) shortage of late 1973/early 1974, due to the OPEC-caused oil crisis and exploding demand for PVC piping in construction. As the story goes, it was hard to get a copy of *Quadrophenia* (and *Billion Dollar Babies* and *Sabbath Bloody Sabbath*) when it first came out. Most U.K. fans had to wait until the band had finished its U.K. tour and left for the United States. Still, it managed a #2 placement on both the U.K. and American charts, held off back home by David Bowie's *Pin Ups* covers album and in the United States by Elton John's *Goodbye Yellow Brick Road*. The album also reached #7 in Australia and #25 in Germany but only #87 in Canada, no doubt in part because the band played only one Canadian date on the tour. Upon release, the album spent thirteen weeks on the Billboard charts and then recharted when the album was remixed and reissued in 1996, achieving a #47 placement and staying on the charts for six weeks.

As should be the case with any self-respecting concept album, *Quadrophenia* found its moderate success through folks loving The Who, seeing the band live, and wanting the *album* as opposed to being driven to the shops by the record's *singles*, none of which did much business. (The #20 placement for "5:15" in the U.K. was one bright spot.) Suffice it to say, this was a band with uncommonly high concert ticket sales in proportion to its record sales. The Who was on MCA in the United States, not the most dynamic and aggressive of imprints, which contributed to only moderately impressive numbers.

Still, in the United States, the album essentially shipped gold, officially certifying on October 29, 1973. It achieved its platinum designation on February 8, 1993, a mass certification day for the band: *Who's Next* was certified triple platinum and *The Who by Numbers* was also certified platinum. Each record of a double album gets counted, so for *Quadrophenia*, gold meant 250,000 copies and platinum 500,000. *Tommy*, also a double, went gold immediately and received both platinum and double platinum certification in 1993. *Quadrophenia* also certified gold in the U.K. and France. The guys have also been presented with industry awards for worldwide sales of the album of more than a million copies.

In 2006, *Q* magazine ranked *Quadrophenia* as the 56th best British album of all time, while over in the States, VH1 called it the 86th best album ever. *Rolling Stone* brought it in at 267th. It was generally well received on both sides of the pond, with the negative reviews of the material seeping in through concert reviews. Most notably, however, both *Melody Maker* and the *NME* put stamps of approval on it, with glowing reviews from Chris Welch and Charles Shaar Murray, respectively.

In modern-day rankings of The Who catalog, *Ultimate Classic Rock* puts *Quadrophenia* 6th out of 13 albums. *Far Out* magazine and Pete Pardo over at *Sea of Tranquility* both put it 3rd out of 12, *Stereogum* ranks it 3rd best out of 11, *NME* has it at #5 out of 10, and *Rolling Stone* has it at #2 of a top 10 list. Aggregator Best Ever Albums puts *Quadrophenia* 2nd after *Who's Next* (almost always the top pick), while the record is ranked as the 5th-best album of 1973, the 43rd-best album of the 1970s, and the 172nd-best album of all time.

Louder Sound puts it at the front on a list of sixteen albums, writing, "The band are on fire. The ensemble interplay that accompanies Roger Daltrey's bullish, career-topping vocal performance is only ever stunning. *Quadrophenia* is Townshend's masterpiece, his most convincing and engaging rock opera by some distance. Based in Mod though eternally relevant, it's bolstered by a vast, cinematic production and is utterly huge in every given sense of the word: in vision, scope, concept and enduring influence."

As for himself, Pete, always one for hyperbole, calls *Quadrophenia* the last great album The Who ever recorded.

WHO GOLD IN ONE DAY

QUADROPHENIA

STEREO

A 2-Record Total Concept Album Produced By The Who.
Includes A 44-Page Booklet. MCA-2-10004

MCA RECORDS

← A print ad from MCA shows off the *Quadrophenia* packaging—and touts its sales achievements.

8

"I'm dressed right for a beach fight"

← Phil Daniels as Jimmy on his
fully extreme, iconic scooter

[*QUADROPHENIA*: THE MOVIE]

When Franc Roddam was trying to secure the job directing what became *Quadrophenia*, his first feature film, Keith gave him a hard time in meetings with The Who. Keith showed up in a Rolls-Royce with an imposing bodyguard in tow, who took it upon himself to laugh at the prospective director's ideas. Keith then suggested (in a boisterous pirate voice) that he and Roddam direct it together. Roddam consented, provided he got to play drums on the next Who album. Six weeks before the first shoot, Keith died, almost scuttling production on the movie altogether, but producers Roy Baird and Bill Curbishley found a way to keep the ball rolling.

Keith was trying to kick the booze and drugs, and the band had just made the *Who Are You* album and the well-received band doc *The Kids Are Alright*. And not long after, there was *McVicar*, which was shown along with *Quadrophenia* on September 14, 1979, at the Toronto Film Festival, made under the auspices of The Who Films Ltd. As it turned out, band manager Curbishley was proving himself adept at the fine art of front-end film financing—he's credited as coproducer along with Baird. And, of course, Pete was always up for a bit of product extension, having watched *Tommy* get a new lease on life as a movie. And then there was Roger, who had found a second career as an actor, even if none of the guys would be turning up in this particular film.

← The lads head out for Brighton. Note that Jimmy's on a less kitted-out scooter than on the previous page.

↑ Phil Daniels as Jimmy with Leslie Ash as Steph

Though Keith was a bit of a problem for Roddam, things went much smoother with Pete, who was already enthusiastic due to Roddam's work on the British hit TV movie *Dummy*. Roddam held his ground when Pete explained his vision for a musical film similar to *Tommy*, with orchestration being a big part of it—in fact, Pete had even brought him some orchestrated *Quadrophenia* pieces to hear. But Roddam told Pete that he was looking to make a "blue-collar street movie" and wanted to use the original music, a suggestion to which Pete readily and graciously agreed. In the end, Roddam's clear stylistic vision, informed by his foundation in documentary filmmaking (including substantial use of handheld cameras), and his admiration for the team assembled ensured that *Quadrophenia* wouldn't come off as a lark made by rock 'n' rollers.

Roddam had been eighteen years old in 1964, and though not a Mod, he was well aware of Mod culture and was even the best man at two Mod weddings. Plus there was already the *Quadrophenia* album, with its thirty meticulously planned photos containing a near storyboard for a future film. Further ensuring success, Roddam made use of a cast—whittled down literally from around one thousand people—that was young and inexpensive, allowing him to prepare them for the shoot over the course of a month. Upward of forty kids were plied with dance lessons in a studio above a strip club and instruction in confident scooter-riding. Another deliberate but subtler instruction happened when shooting began. Roddam wanted them to look like easy friends, so he had them hang out like a gang, go see bands, get to know one another, wear the Mod clothes, and party like Mods—this was definitely a rock 'n' roll movie being made, and as shooting began, the late-night carousing kept going and was even encouraged.

In this light, nineteen-year-old Phil Daniels, still living at home with his mom and dad, was the perfect pick to play Jimmy. He's now a famed actor with a storied career, but even then, he had been through the Anna Scher Theatre School and the National Youth Theater and was skilled at improvising. This came in handy at numerous spots throughout the film where he put in brilliant ad-libbed performances, many of them a mix of angry and exasperated. This was a godsend to Roddam, as the writing of the script—by himself, Pete, Dave Humphries, and Martin Stellman (an actual Mod, he says, but without a scooter)—was a rushed affair, barely a month elapsing between the start of it and the first shoot. Roddam had signed the papers to work on the film on June 13, 1978, and they were shooting by September 26.

Pete liked Daniels' look as well—punky, not particularly attractive, unexpected, and resembling Terry Kennett from the photographs back in 1973. Johnny Rotten had also tried out for the part and had tested admirably, but the team's insurance company wouldn't back him. Nor was Curbishley too hot on Rotten, remembering when he used to call The Who boring old farts. In the end, Daniels was a brilliant choice, balancing pilled-up, sleep-deprived pathos with both empathy and sympathy, providing a sense that Jimmy's surging teenage hormones are as intoxicating as anything he's taking.

None other than Gordon "Sting" Sumner was enlisted to play Ace Face, the top Mod in the film, by definition the Face above the Tickets and the Numbers, the leader of the

← Gordon "Sting" Sumner as Ace Face

↑ Jimmy and Steph in the famous alleyway scene. Meanwhile, there's a riot in the streets.

pack that Jimmy so dearly aspires to match. Priceless in this regard is Jimmy's glowing adoration of Ace when they're in court and Ace offers to write a check on the spot for the fine the judge has just administered—Daniels' got no lines, but the sense of fandom he paints on Jimmy's face is beautiful. As for Sting, the cast has fond memories of the peroxide blond playing for them, on the guitar, songs from the imminent first Police record *Outlandos d'Amour*. Although no rock star yet, six years later, Sting was a household name and played the lead in a Roddam-directed horror film called *The Bride*. (Phil Daniels also showed up in a lesser role.)

To make the film, the record company had fronted £1 million and told them to get on with it, and that's what they did. The team worked its way through the funds fairly quickly (but not irresponsibly) given the complicated riot shoot and general professionalism of the film, including the deft scooter-riding scenes, the wardrobe, and the struggle to make everything look like 1964, the odd Ford Capri from the 1970s notwithstanding.

Most harrowing was the scene in which Jimmy's scooter goes over the cliff. (Can you spot the suddenly missing windscreen? Plus, the lights on his scooter, a Rally 200 disguised as a Vespa GS, are from the 1970s.) This was mathematically worked out and tested using sandbags, but when it came to the shoot, the scooter flew twice as far as expected and almost knocked the helicopter that was being used to film the scene out of the sky. Also in this opening sequence, we see Jimmy walking away from the cliff. In the story, Pete kept the question of whether Jimmy commits suicide somewhat ambiguous, although any cursory look will reveal he doesn't. What Roddam does with this opening sequence strikes the same hopeful tone, although the idea of Jimmy flying a scooter off a huge cliff is a significant change from Pete putting him soaked and freezing out on some rocks in the ocean. In any event, as Roddam sagely put it, the scene—not to mention the wider record and the film—is "symbolic as an end, not of life, but a way of life."

↓ A bad day for Jimmy just got worse. But it all proves to be part and parcel of some much-needed personal reflection and growth.

↑ The iconic cast shot used in a number of promotional pieces

The rest of the plot is surprisingly true to the album, with many extra memorable scenes stuck in. Jimmy and Steph stealing away into a narrow alley to have sex has not only made that alley a famed Mod tourist attraction, but also, Roddam quips, it's the only sex scene in film history where everybody's got their clothes on. There's also more made of the mind games between Jimmy and Steph and her other potential suitors. This leads to a great scene where Jimmy, trying to impress, one-ups a stiffly dancing Ace Face by darting upstairs, dancing up on a balcony, and taking a huge leap into the crowd. Incidentally, Sting's gray suit here, not particularly Mod looking, cost £500 to make, an enormous sum in 1979. There's also extra detail concerning attacks by Rockers, coupled with Mod retaliation. Pete at one point became concerned that the film was too violent and at risk of losing his spiritual message. In fact, *Quadrophenia* got an X rating when it began showing in theaters, meaning that seventeen-year-old Mark Wingate, who played Jimmy's buddy Dave in the film, was too young to see it.

Other liberties taken included Jimmy's occupation. In the booklet included with the original album, he's shown emptying trash cans, which is corroborated by the intro essay although not specified in the lyrics. In the movie, he works in the mail room of an advertising firm. There's also the extra scene where the guys are ripped off with fake pills from a mobbed-up dealer. They retaliate by vandalizing his car, which, granted, lines up three pictures in the original booklet. One cheeky feature has Jimmy and his buddies go nuts

QUADROPHENIA THE MOVIE ... a trip that will wake you up and shake you up
QUADROPHENIA THE MOVIE ... a pocketful of dreams was their way of life
QUADROPHENIA THE MOVIE ... a condition of today
QUADROPHENIA THE MOVIE ... produced by 'The Who'

QUADROPHENIA

THE WHO FILMS Present A CURBISHLEY BAIRD PRODUCTION **QUADROPHENIA**
Musical Directors ROGER DALTREY • JOHN ENTWISTLE • PETE TOWNSHEND
Screenplay by DAVE HUMPHRIES • MARTIN STELLMAN • FRANC RODDAM • Produced by ROY BAIRD & BILL CURBISHLEY
Directed by FRANC RODDAM • A POLYTEL FILM • [DD] DOLBY STEREO

QUADROPHENIA

una forma de vida

PHIL DANIELS · MARK WINGETT · PHILIP DAVIS · LESLIE ASH

Directores Musicales: ROGER DALTREY · JOHN ENTWISTLE · PETE TOWNSHEND   Guión de DAVE HUMPHRIES · MARTIN STELLMAN · FRANC RODDAM

Una Producción de ROY BAIRD & BILL CURBISHLEY · Un Film de FRANC RODDAM

DISTRIBUCION
INTERCINE S.A.

Banda Sonora en Discos y Cintas polydor

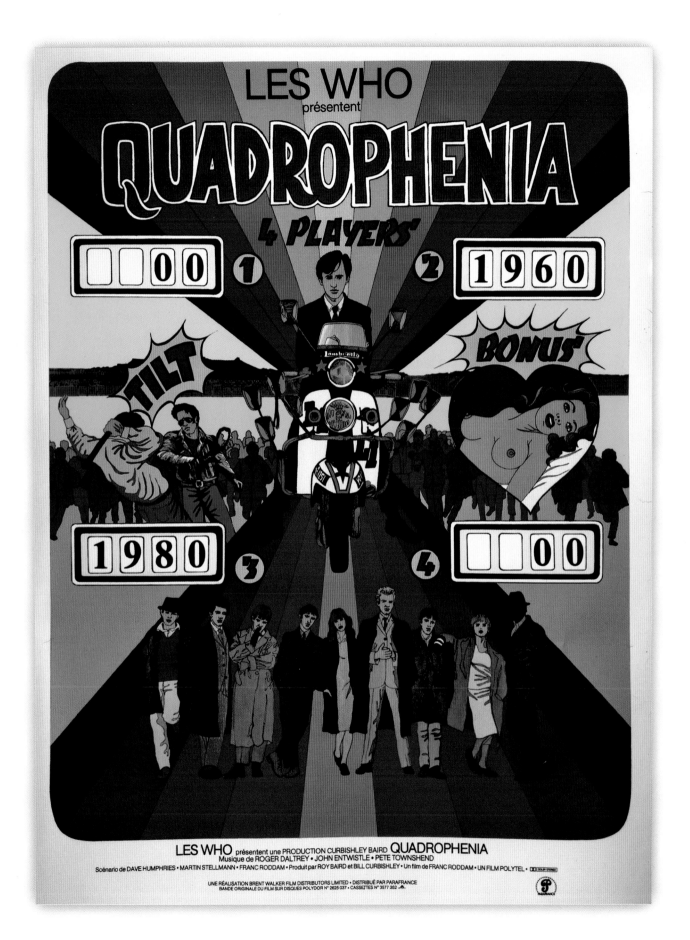

ハートブレイクなんてクソくらえ
俺は風だ——
ドラッグやって
マシーンで吹っ飛び
ロック&ロールでも聞きながら
背中の翼で翔べばいい。

ばらさ
春青の
光

デジタルリマスター版

QUADROPHENIA

PHIL DANIELS MARK WINGETT PHILIP DAVIS LESLIE ASH GARRY COOPER TOYAH WILLCOX
'STING' TREVOR LAIRD KATE WILLIAMS MICHAEL ELPHICK KIM NEVE RAY WINSTONE GARY SHAIL
PRODUCERS ROY BAIRD BILL CURBISHLEY EXECUTIVE PRODUCERS THE WHO
DIRECTOR FRANC RODDAM SCREENPLAY DAVE HUMPHRIES MARTIN STELLMAN FRANC RODDAM
MUSICAL DIRECTORS JOHN ENTWISTLE PETE TOWNSHEND
Design ©2006 Universal Studios. All Rights Reserved. Film ©1979 Who Films, Inc. All Rights Reserved.

sarabaseishun2019.com

to "My Generation" at a house party, even though the movie's set in 1964 and the single came out in 1965. There was a bit of controversy when a sex scene between a Black male and a white girl was cut due to worries about the film being banned in South America and the American South, almost prompting a strike by the cast.

All told, *Quadrophenia* turned out to be an accomplished, serious piece of work and was well received by critics—it was released in Japan as well, renamed *The Pain of Living*. Now, decades later, past its life as a film into the nascent time-shifting era of VCRs and its availability as a physical product, there's now YouTube, meaning that anybody can watch it with the click of a few keystrokes in various formats: full-length, as clips, discussed and reviewed, or even formally celebrated through documentaries. In this context, the film did most of the heavy lifting versus the album or indeed any other project about Mod culture in terms of directly and relentlessly documenting many aspects of Mod life. The fact that it was a likable movie with universal appeal as a film about the hard graft of being a teenager only helped.

For those serious about it, there's the physical product, including the initial DVD from 1999 and the cleaned-up (but slightly shorter) version from two years later. Then there's the expanded, restored, and remastered issue from August 2006, featuring a one-hour documentary and commentary from Roddam, Daniels, and Leslie Ash, who played to perfection the wily, independent, and desirable Steph. She was only eighteen but had acted since fifteen, making her one of the most seasoned kids flung into this situation. In the end, it is her performance—and Daniels' anguished reaction to it at every turn—that perhaps points us in the direction of the original "Love, Reign o'er Me" message Pete wanted retained from the album and poured into the frames of this cultural landmark of a film.

Following upon soundtrack albums for *Tommy* in 1975 and *The Kids Are Alright* in the summer of 1979, here comes a double album to accompany the *Quadrophenia* film, on October 5, 1979, offering as many delightful odds 'n' sods as *Odds & Sods* did back in 1974.

First off, Polydor did a nice job with the packaging, offering a handsome, full-color shot of Jimmy on the front, a back cover nicely similar to that of the original album, and a sweeping gatefold shot of the cast inside. The two original vinyl records were housed in color-printed sleeves featuring stills from the movie but also snuck in shots of Phil Daniels with Pete and with Roger, plus a stand-alone shot of John. This was emblematic of John's status as music director on the project, the Ox working closely over the course of a month with Franc Roddam once the film had gone through a final edit to sort the music out for the record. Scattered about the inner sleeves are various pills in illustrated form, giving the graphics a Hipgnosis-type look. The packaging design was credited to Richard Evans, who worked for Hipgnosis and had done things for The Who since 1976 and after this project as well. Even the labels on the actual vinyl were custom, all the credits clumped onto two of them, with simple graphics on the other two.

Once into the grooves, John's involvement becomes material. Past the "I Am the Sea" intro, we get a version of "The Real Me" on which John switched in new bass parts, also bringing Roger up in the mix and taking the artiness out of the ending, changing it to a standard Who bash-up. From here we get seven more remixed versions of original *Quadrophenia* songs to finish off the first record, creating an imagining of a single LP version of the album. Aside from "I Am the Sea," side

one features all the highest-profile tracks, closing off with "I'm One" (featuring added piano), "5:15," and a "Love, Reign o'er Me," reblessed with a profusion of pretty orchestration and the original kerranging band windup removed and replaced with a civilized version, again sweetened with strings.

Over to side two, it's "Bell Boy," "I've Had Enough," "Helpless Dancer" (at twenty-one seconds, in name only!), and "Doctor [sic] Jimmy," with the latter missing the opening and closing sound effects. All told, it's a case of original sequence be damned, with the deletions consisting of "Quadrophenia," "Cut My Hair," "The Dirty Jobs," "Helpless Dancer," "Is It in My Head?", "Sea and Sand," "Drowned," and "The Rock." One additional track, "The Punk and the Godfather," shows up on the second piece of vinyl.

Part of the reason there were so many tweaks to the songs and sequencing stemmed from the fact that MCA, who had the rights to and was still selling the original album, had pressured Polydor over the duplication, with Polydor having to somewhat appease MCA that the soundtrack album would be appreciably changed from the original so as not to cannibalize sales.

Side three of *Quadrophenia* 2.0 begins with "Zoot Suit," the A side of the band's first single, recording as The High Numbers. The song was written by the band's first manager, Peter Meaden, to whom the album is dedicated. (Meaden died of a drug overdose on July 29, 1978, at the age of thirty-six.) "Zoot Suit" is more purist Mod than even "My Generation," mixing The Beatles with soul melodies to create a nascent garage rock anthem less than two minutes long, topped with lyrics that are historic for establishing the Mod credo in song.

ORIGINAL MOTION PICTURE SOUNDTRACK FROM THE WHO FILM **QUADROPHENIA**

Polydor

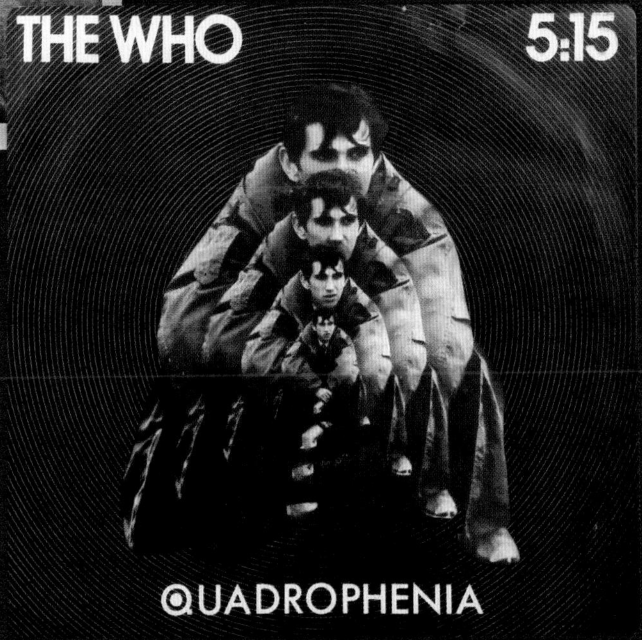

THE WHO 5:15

QUADROPHENIA

145

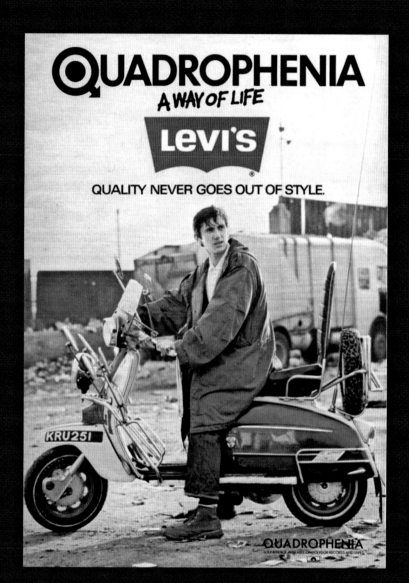

↑ Jimmy unwittingly pitches Levi's—togs arguably better associated with the rival Rockers.

→ The film soundtrack leaned heavily on American soul, R&B, and garage rock.

Next comes a cover of Tommy Tucker's "Hi-Heel Sneakers" from 1963. This is performed by an obscure band of teenagers called Cross Section, who appear briefly in the film as the band onstage when Dave and Steph are dancing. Kenney Jones makes his debut as The Who's new drummer on "Get Out and Stay Out," a short semi-ska song without much to say beyond the title, which signifies Jimmy's parents kicking him out of the house. Pete first demoed this on November 12, 1972, and decided against including it on the original album because it featured Jimmy's parents too strongly too early on the record.

Then we're into the ebullient, delightful "Four Faces," a dropped song from the original *Quadrophenia* sessions and thus drummed by Keith, no longer with us at that point. Over a series of irresistible piano pop passages reminiscent of 10cc or ELO or Supertramp, we get an inventive mathematical exposition on Jimmy's four-part personality, how there's four of everything as he goes about his mixed-up day. Conjecturing, had it been included on the original album, "Four Faces" might have been a hit. But then again it sits outside the record's serious tone, echoing Pete's reservations about Keith's "Bell Boy" performance.

Left undeveloped for the original album from Pete's original demos were songs like "We Close Tonight," "You Came Back," "Get Inside," "Anymore," and "Ambition." "Joker James" turned out to be the one proper song from the batch singled out for working up with Kenney, and The Who performed it like a Mod revival band. At the lyric end, however, there's little real connection to the story. As Pete explains, the unifying theme across the omitted songs is Jimmy's childhood, but he decided that the story would be better if we met Jimmy as a teenager, already embroiled in teenage problems. Still, we can be thankful that one of these was rescued for the soundtrack album.

Side four offers up seven songs representing a Mod playlist pre-Who or concurrent with The Who, but not back to the roots of Mod in modern jazz. Frankly, it's a bit of a letdown, because these are all classic popular pop songs, anything but a deep dive. What's more, a slog through these hugely recognizable pop culture staples leaves the listener more confused about what Mods danced to at the end of the album than they were going in.

Upon release, the soundtrack album reached #23 on the U.K. charts and #46 on Billboard, and the single "5:15" backed with "I'm One" promoted the album across many territories (the A side managed a #45 placement on the Billboard Hot 100). A 1993 issue of the album on CD culled just The Who material, kicking off with "I'm the Face," followed by "Zoot Suit," and then into all The Who songs in the same order as the 1979 album. A 2000 CD reissue offered the same songs and the same running order as the entire 1979 double album, adding "I'm the Face" at the very end of the single-disc package. Most fun is the Record Store Day issue from 2017, limited to eight hundred copies and pressed on 180-gram parka-green vinyl!

Remarkably, both the *Quadrophenia* album of 1973 and the *Quadrophenia* film of 1979 just might have less to do with the Mod revival than what Pete Meaden, Chris Stamp, Kit Lambert, Richard Barnes, and the members of The Who had brought to the table back in 1964 and 1965. It's Paul Weller who lit the spark of revival, quietly a full-on Mod teenager and then suddenly, at nineteen, fronting The Jam, the first Mod band in a dozen years. And that had nothing to do with a movie that wasn't out yet and less to do with The Who album than a love for the original magic era. It was right there on the front cover of The Jam's first album, *In the City*, with Weller, Bruce Foxton, and Rick Buckler in the suits and ties and haircuts, moving the culture on from punk to a place few understood outside of themselves and the odd Mod they'd spot in the crowd or on the street.

As the legend goes, neither The Jam's fortunes nor Mod culture was moved forward by the ill-received second album, *This Is the Modern World*, but then on November 3, 1978, the band delivered *All Mod Cons*—standing for "all modern conveniences"—and the new Mods had their masterpiece, their biblical text. Weller had both widened his palette and sharpened his songwriting, tapping specifically into a Ray Davies Mod dimension about the working class. This was an important point, because the growing gaggle of new Mods had become disillusioned with the commercialization of punk music and punk fashion, dismissing it as suddenly middle class.

A milestone moment came on May 1, 1979, when bands inspired by The Jam assembled at a pub called the Bridge House in Canning Town, East London, and scampered through some of their tight power pop numbers. Recorded and released to the public, the record is called *Mods Mayday '79*. Financed by the pub, it features Squire, Beggar, The Mods, Small Hours, The Merton Parkas, and Secret Affair. Only Secret Affair became one of a small clutch of bands viewable with the naked eye as they orbited the life-giving force at the center of this Mod-revival universe known as The Jam.

Meanwhile, back in the land of the dinosaurs, the now greatly extended Who family, incredibly and with no awareness or ulterior motive, began shooting *Quadrophenia* just as *All Mod Cons* hit the shops. Oblivious to this Mod trend that was still very much underground, this was a case of The Who just doing business, getting on with a project that sounded interesting, working a formula they'd worked with *Tommy*. Furthermore, it wasn't as if there was a Mod revival in 1974 or 1975 after the original album, nor was there one a few years back or indeed at any point *before* the *Quadrophenia* album. This was just a case of "let's make another one of Pete's albums into a movie."

The timeline began with *In the City* and grew (modestly) exponentially through *All Mod Cons* and *Mod Mayday '79*, with the summer of 1979 living on as the golden era, the peak of excitement for the revival, driven by weekly music paper *Sounds* dependably documenting the scene. The Jam then issued another classic in *Setting Sons* on November 16, 1979, two weeks after the *Quadrophenia* film emerged.

Also significantly, The Jam took two new Mod revival bands on tour, The Chords and Purple Hearts. They also tapped as support Secret Affair, who got its own Arista Records subimprint, I-Spy. The band issued *Glory Boys* in 1979, *Behind Closed Doors* in 1980, and *Business as Usual* in 1982. Chris Parry emerged as a Mod record producer, working first with The Jam but also The Chords, Purple Hearts, Back to Zero, and Long Tall Shorty. At the same time, there was a profusion of Mod fanzines like *Maximum Speed*, as well as the two-tone ska revival, with significant crossover into Mod. In fact, a handful of those bands, like The Selecter, The Beat, The Specials, Bad Manners, and Madness, eclipsed the success of any Mod revival band but The Jam. As for other known quantities, there were The Lambrettas and The Merton Parkas, the latter of which managed a Top 40 hit with a song called "You Need Wheels." And yes, accompanying all of this, we saw many scooters with many mirrors and the full range of the fashion seen in the sixties, with no real deviation from the mean.

And where did the *Quadrophenia* film fit in all this? Mods were smart enough to understand that the movie wasn't put into production to cash in on the Mod revival, but at the same time, the more perceptive fans surmised that the movie would drive a stake through the revival. They'd seen what happened to punk and knew the art of subcultures well, having watched how these things ebb and flow. As soon as a subculture becomes mainstream, the originals balk. There'd been Teddy Boys, Rockers, Mods, and Skinheads of various ilk, and they'd all replayed the Brighton Beach riots over all manner of bank holidays through the decade, chased one another in the streets, or clashed at gigs. As it turned out, *Quadrophenia* '79—just like *Quadrophenia* '73—didn't have the power to start or end anything. Rather, the Mod revival was just there; it was appreciated enough, and it petered away, mostly, one might conjecture, from a lack of good bands.

If anything lasting or impactful has come out of it, it surely wasn't the blip of a revival in Los Angeles or the evolution in American skinny-tie new wave, fronted by The Cars, The Knack, and The Romantics. Rather, for maximum piercing of the pop culture fabric, we must look to mid-1990s Britpop and the immense success of Oasis, Blur, Pulp, and The Stone Roses, plus lesser but equally Mod-adjacent acts like Menswear, Supergrass, and Suede. Granted, there's range across that list, but there are multiple ties, not least of which is Noel Gallagher's very public friendship with the Modfather himself, Paul Weller.

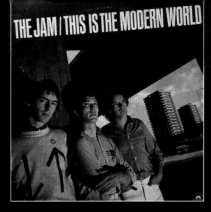

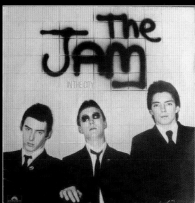

↗ The Jam (top right) were the most prominent of the Mod revival groups, joined by the likes of Secret Affair (center right), The Specials (bottom right), and Merton Parkas (bottom left).

9

> " I pick up phones and hear my history "

← Live in 1979 with new drummer Kenney Jones

[THE WHO POST-*QUADROPHENIA*]

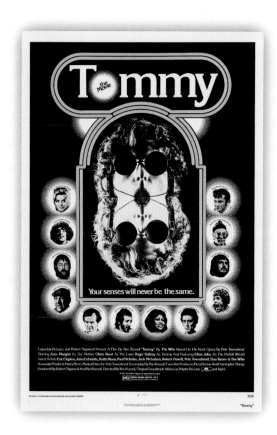

↗ The Who in the 1975 Ken Russell–directed film version of *Tommy*

Pete has stated that giving Roger, John, and Keith jobs to do was his way of trying to save The Who. If that's the case, *Quadrophenia*, for all the pressures of its birthing, wouldn't be a patch on its postproduction period. Even before the live presentation of the problematic album was carried out and then unceremoniously dispensed with, it was all-hands-on-deck for the film version of *Tommy*. That meant pretty much redoing all the music in-house, not to mention filming, which took place marbled among concert dates in the first half of 1974.

The effort turned out to be worth it, and both the movie and the two-LP soundtrack album, out simultaneously in March 1975, were big hits. The film, starring Ann-Margret, Oliver Reed, Tina Turner, Elton John, Jack Nicholson, Eric Clapton, and Roger Daltrey, made back $34 million, ten times what it cost, and the album was RIAA-certified as gold.

Yet it turned out that keeping Roger and Keith in the spotlight with flash friends wasn't helping the band. Roger hadn't been happy with Pete's guitar playing, Keith was still spiraling downward with pills and booze, and Pete himself was disillusioned, wanting to express himself through solo work, which is essentially what the next record, *The Who by Numbers*, felt like; the lyrics were often personal to the point of confessional. But then there was "Squeeze Box," nearly a novelty song but a surefire hit for the band. Album-opener "Slip Kid" was issued as the second and last single but to relative indifference, even if over time its reputation has grown. Decades later, both songs are classic rock staples, and the wider album is viewed with more fondness than it was met with back in the mid-1970s, when there was a growing sense that the industry was getting a bit tired of The Who and all the extracurricular reasons the guys were showing up in the papers.

← Pinball wizard Kenneth Thomas "Kenney" Jones in 1974. Jones played with Small Faces and Faces before joining The Who following Keith Moon's death in 1978.

Most of 1975 wasn't toured and most of 1976 was. Both 1977 and 1978 saw but a single show each year, filmed specialty concerts needed for the band documentary *The Kids Are Alright*. The most pertinent problem was Keith, whose percussive skills had further deteriorated along with his health. Still, after a year spent giving his family some attention (and watching with amusement London's punk rock explosion), Pete called the guys back to work, somehow managing to get an album out of Keith.

Who Are You "had enough" (to quote a song title on the record) to keep a substantial wedge of fans and critics in the positive column. More suddenly turned up on the approving side after Keith's death three weeks after the record's August 18, 1978, arrival in stores. The shocking loss of Keith (despite being pictured on the cover in a chair that said "Not to Be Taken Away") seems almost inevitable given his condition during the sessions, not to mention the bad vibes all around. Pete had sliced his hand on a smashed window during a fight with his parents, and Roger was doing a number on his own hands, punching producer Glyn Johns over his vocal mix. Roger also had to undergo throat surgery during the sessions. Nobody was enthusiastic about the way the record had gone, and fans groused about the band being out of touch, specifically pointing out the profusion of synthesizers from Pete.

By the middle of 1979, The Who was back with a new drummer in Kenney Jones from Small Faces and The Faces, and the band toured the rest of the year hard. This helped turn "Who Are You" into an enormous and beloved song in The Who catalog and its source album into one of the band's most successful sellers at double platinum. The next three years were productive, resulting in 1981's *Face Dances* and 1982's *It's Hard*, both

garnering many complaints but again doing enough to keep the band in the good graces of the music industry. *Face Dances* went platinum, aided and abetted by "You Better You Bet," while *It's Hard* managed gold, "Eminence Front" growing in stature over time to the point where it's now one of the band's most recognized songs.

Further casting a pall on The Who's future after Keith's passing was the band's concert at Riverfront Stadium in Cincinnati, Ohio, on December 3, 1979. Eleven concertgoers were trampled to death in a "festival seating" nightmare gone wrong. If any good was to come out of the situation, it was a comprehensive rethink of general-admission ticket policies, with safety rules and procedures (not always adhered to) put in place from that tragic day forward.

Amid the tragedy, along with Pete's crossing into heroin addiction and band infighting over Kenney Jones as Keith's replacement, there were disagreements over touring. Pete wanted to hang it up and make solo records, while John wanted to tour regularly, happy with playing the old hits. Meanwhile, Roger was busy with *McVicar*, both a successful film and solo album, and there was enough going on with *The Kids Are Alright* and *Quadrophenia*—both films and double soundtrack albums—to give the illusion that the kids were all right.

They weren't. The band famously mounted its 1982 "farewell" tour, supported by The Clash, before Pete bought himself and Kenney out of The Who's contract for another studio album and announced his quitting of the band.

Pete proceeded to keep his word for quite a spell. The Who played Live Aid in 1985 before announcing a twenty-five-year reunion tour for 1989, notably without Kenney.

→ Concertgoers and a policeman stand with a pile of shoes and clothing that were left after a crowd surged toward the doors to Cincinnati's Riverfront Coliseum to get into the band's ill-fated 1979 performance in the Ohio city. Eleven fans were killed in the tragedy.

NÜRNBERG OPEN AIR
1. SEPT. '79
Lippmann + Rau / Scheller present
THE WHO
CHEAP TRICK.   AC/DC.
MIRIAM MAKEBA.
SCORPIONS.
STEVE GIBBONS BAND.
ZANKI & BAND.

Samstag 1.Sept.   Karten DM 30,-- + Vorverkaufsgebühr
NÜRNBERG Zeppelinfeld   DM 35,-- Tageskasse
Beginn 14.00 Uhr Einlass 10.00 Uhr   bei allen bek. Vorverkaufsstellen

HARVEY GOLDSMITH BY ARRANGEMENT WITH TRINIFOLD LTD PRESENTS

The Who
AND FRIENDS ROAR IN!

WEMBLEY STADIUM
SATURDAY 18th August
Gates open 2pm—
Concert ends 10pm
Tickets £8 inc. VAT in advance
ON SALE FROM 10am
SATURDAY 7th JULY

SCHLITZ ROCKS AMERICA
AND PROUDLY PRESENTS

THE WHO
WITH SPECIAL GUEST STARS
THE CLASH
FRI. OCT. 29 3PM
COLISEUM
Schlitz - The Taste That Rocks America

Simon Phillips, who had proven himself with Pete on his solo work, filled in. But that was it until 1996, when the band returned to the road to support the newly released deluxe CD issue of *Quadrophenia*. Along the way, in 1990, just after the first reunion tour, the band was inducted into the Rock and Roll Hall of Fame, ushered in by U2. Also on the Cleveland shrine dance card that year were fellow Mod squadders The Kinks.

A series of charity gigs marked the end of the decade. The year 2000 was a particularly heavy touring year. Gone were the big ensemble troupes bringing concept albums to life. Instead, the band worked as a five-piece. Pete, Roger, and John were joined by Zak Starkey on drums and John "Rabbit" Bundrick on keyboards, both carryovers from the *Quadrophenia* tour configuration. A milestone show in Who lore is the performance at the October 2001 Concert for New York City following the terrorist attacks of September 11. With Jon Carin switched in on keyboards in place of Rabbit, the band played "Who Are You," "Baba O'Riley," "Behind Blue Eyes," and "Won't Get Fooled Again," the latter being one of the galvanizing highlight moments for the first responders in the crowd that magical night.

↑ The Live Aid concert for famine relief at Wembley Stadium, London, July 13, 1985

←← Germany, 1979. The windmill still works.

↑ The Quiet One on stage at the MGM Grand, Las Vegas, for an October 29, 1999, reunion-era concert staged by new Internet company Pixelon.com

On July 27, 2002, the Quiet One was gone; John passed away in a Las Vegas hotel room just as the band was to embark on a U.S. tour. The show must go on, and it did. John's son, Christopher, gave the band his blessing, and Pino Palladino stepped in. The band did not tour the following year, and 2004 was light, with two new songs in "Real Good Looking Boy" and "Old Red Wine" added to a compilation called *Then and Now*. The former was a tribute to Elvis Presley, and the latter was a tribute to the Ox. In 2005, Pete and Roger played one show as a duet and also "Who Are You" and "Won't Get Fooled Again" at Live 8, full band, in London's Hyde Park.

But then the machine cranked up again. In October 2006, The Who issued *Endless Wire*, a confounding yet arresting collection of short pieces of music and proper songs, featuring recurring themes, a dynamic spectrum of arrangements, the *Wire & Glass* mini opera, and versions of the album with alternate track lists and bonus material. Plus, *Wire & Glass* was issued as a stand-alone EP, the narrative complicated further by the confluence of the songs with Pete's theatrical work, *The Boy Who Heard Music*.

Ambitious touring ensued over the following three years, including visits to Japan, Australia, and New Zealand. In 2010, Pete and Roger played acoustic at a press conference in advance of their half-time performance at Super Bowl XLIV, for which they cooked up a typical action-packed medley. After a March 30 show that year in support of the Teenage Cancer Trust, that was it until 2011, which featured a lone set of four songs in support of the Killing Cancer charity.

→ Pete takes off during the Live 8 Concert in Hyde Park, London, July 2, 2005. The concert, held simultaneously in many cities around the world, including Paris, Berlin, Philadelphia, and Rome, was intended to call attention to world poverty ahead of the following week's G8 meeting in Scotland.

↑ The Who perform during halftime at Super Bowl XLIV at Sun Life Stadium, Miami, Florida, February 7, 2010.

In 2012 and 2013, *Quadrophenia* in all its Mod glory was back. A North American and European tour supported the second upgrade of the album. Chris Stainton, co-keyboardist with Pete on the original album, proved an exciting addition to the team. A good ol' regular set list was the subject of tour dates through 2014, 2015, and 2016, and the band played for the first time ever in the United Arab Emirates and for only the second time ever at the Glastonbury Festival. At this point, the Who celebrated its fiftieth anniversary and had a new album called *The Who Hits 50!*, which included a strident yet toe-tapping fresh track called "Be Lucky." *Tommy* was the focus of a short U.K. tour at the beginning of 2017, after which the band transitioned to North America, playing an ambitious set list of hits, with more talk all the time of this finally being the end of the road.

But our *Quadrophenia*-anchored story has a happy surprise ending—on December 6, 2019, out of nowhere Pete and Roger returned with a brand-new album called *Who*. The release was quite unexpected after an ambitious stack of tour dates throughout the year and Pete's and Roger's ages, seventy-three and seventy-five, respectively. The *Who* album just might go down in history as the most effusively received record from the band since *Who's Next* and *Tommy*.

The advance single was "Ball and Chain" (a reworking of an obscure Pete solo track called "Guantanamo"), but it's the opener "All This Music Must Fade" that will wind up making the lasting impact. In the song, Pete amusingly and yet with a trace of impending mortality puts all of the music making that he and his compatriots have done in perspective. The lyric augments what has been called "the long goodbye" from Roger and Pete, namely all this regular touring since apparently calling it quits back in 1982 and only three new studio albums along the way. As Roger roars with power, "All this music will fade, just like the edge of a blade." Somewhere in that simile lies the wisdom that the old Who—jostled by John and Keith at the rhythm end but actually aggressive to a man—indeed once cut like a knife.

Arriving full circle, *Quadrophenia*, the record we've celebrated throughout this book, with its dense, thorny, and even clumpy sound collages, is evidence of The Who playing this way not only for the last time but most confidently and deliberately, maintaining that density and attendant intensity through four sides of original vinyl. No question, *Quadrophenia* was a cause for concern at the time, but as those concerns, anxieties,

↓ Roger and Pete perform during the "12-12-12" benefit concert for victims of Superstorm Sandy at Madison Square Garden, New York City, December 12, 2012.

↑ The Who on the Pyramid Stage during the Glastonbury Festival at Worthy Farm, Somerset, June 28, 2015

→→ Wembley Stadium, London, March 13, 2019

and animosities have faded over the years, band and critic and fan alike have grown to embrace the record fully, celebrating it together on two major tours decades after it might have been forgotten as a concept album not worth learning. *Quadrophenia* indeed proved to be worth learning. Despite Pete's culturally interesting placement of the tale within the Mod movement of 1964, at the heart of it is the story of what it's like to be a teenager. And, in the spirit of hope, how one may come out of it on the other side wiser, more serious, and, as Pete artfully gets across, perhaps even spiritually transformed.

THE WHO & QUADROPHENIA

The first time *Quadrophenia* received a full airing since 1974 turned out to be a very special occasion indeed. Pete was approached to bring his rock opera out of retirement for the Prince's Trust Charity Concert of 1996 staged in Hyde Park on June 29. He originally planned to perform the suite acoustic with film backing, but thanks to sponsorship funds from Vespa, he went full band with distinguished guests, including Phil Daniels, Stephen Fry, and David Gilmour, who played the bus driver and also blessed the performance with additional guitar. The new Who band was big enough, but backing vocalists and a horn section filled it out further.

The momentous experience served as the basis for an only slightly pared down, more conventional Who tour of the album, beginning with a six-night stand at Madison Square Garden in New York in mid-July. More than eighty-five thousand fans got to witness the event. Smartly, this was taking place in conjunction with the first deluxe reissue of *Quadrophenia* on CD, remixed and remastered. The band picked up again for an ambitious U.S. tour in October and November, finishing the year with two Earl's Court shows and one in Manchester. Mainland Europe followed in April and May 1997, with the band back in America to close out the tour in July and August. As for the set list, all of *Quadrophenia* was played on this tour, followed by an encore in which three to five Who hits were performed, usually including "Won't Get Fooled Again," "Behind Blue Eyes," and "Who Are You," and maybe "I Can't Explain" and "Substitute." The Dayton, Ohio, stop on November 4, 1996, can be seen and heard on the *Tommy and Quadrophenia Live* DVD box set issued in 2005.

On March 10, 2010, the band played *Quadrophenia* in its entirety once again as part of a series of concerts in support of the Teenage Cancer Trust. This was followed by a 2012–2013 tour called *Quadrophenia and More*, where the album was played in its entirety but without guest stars. The core band at this point consisted of Pete and Roger, with Simon Townshend on second guitar and additional vocals, Pino Palladino on bass, and Zak Starkey on drums. In tribute to the fallen members of the original Who, video footage was used showing John playing his "5:15" bass solo and Keith singing "Bell Boy." Like last time, this tour took place with product to push, namely a new deluxe version of the album on CD along with the director's cut box set consisting of four CDs, a DVD, a bonus reproduction "5:15"/"Water" single, various paper goods, and a hardcover book featuring extensive liner notes from Pete.

There have also been numerous theatrical presentations of *Quadrophenia* beginning in 2005. The most extensive and formal was the U.K. touring troupe of 2009, for which one of the four Jimmys, Ryan O'Donnell, was nominated for the TMA Award for Best Performance in a Musical.

On June 8, 2015, as part of The Who's fiftieth anniversary celebrations, Pete and his partner, Rachel Fuller, saw the release of *Classic Quadrophenia*, orchestrated by Rachel (and Martin Batchelar on three tracks), performed by the Royal Philharmonic Orchestra and conducted by Robert Ziegler. The sessions took place in October the previous year at Air Studios in London. On vocals were the London Oriana Choir, lead by choirmaster Dominic Peckham. Opera tenor and stage actor Alfie Boe provided the lion's share of the lead vocals.

→→ Madison Square Garden, New York City, July 18, 1996

Pete jumped in for a cameo on "The Punk and the Godfather" and played a little guitar, Billy Idol sang on four tracks, and Phil Daniels appeared on two.

Pete's original plan was to have Rachel come up with a pliable score that would serve as the approved basis for any future productions of *Quadrophenia*, musical to music, and whatever else any other "entrepreneur" might dream up. As Pete puts it, the initial thought was to come up with nothing more than "a folio, really, just a book of music." Fuller then set up a high-tech home studio (assisted in the construction by Hans Zimmer) and, working with Martin Batchelar, came up with a score that turned out to be plush enough to serve as building blocks of what is pretty much a traditional album of opera music worthy of release on the esteemed Deutsche Grammophon classical label.

The resulting album represents the final grace note played by *Quadrophenia* to date, with the entire suite of products and performances since 1973 now rivaling in abundance and quality what the band managed to do with *Tommy*. Which will ring and bring joy with the most resonance over the ensuing decades is anyone's guess, but nonetheless, we must thank Pete and the guys for walking through fire and delivering them both.

↖↖ "Thank you and I bid you a good night." San Diego, February 5, 2013

←← Classic and classical Pete at London's Royal Albert Hall, July 5, 2015

167

collectibles

Consider this the accompanying text cards for a glass display case of *Quadrophenia* curios across a number of collecting categories, excluding variants of the original album itself, which are dealt with in a separate sidebar. I've not gone down the road of pricing, given the vast range at any point in time, further fluctuations over time, and the wild card of condition. Plus, auction results tend to reflect the individual psychologies of a buyer and seller, not to mention those of the unsuccessful bidders that month or week or day. I'd also like to point out that we've just scratched the surface concerning the "5:15" single and *Quadrophenia* film poster variants, especially the latter, where delightful creative liberties were taken across the many territories in which the film was feted.

Quadrophenia color one-sheet advertisement with live shot, 1973, Italy.

Quadrophenia two-sided square card store display, 1973, South Africa.

Bill Graham Presents in San Francisco The Who, Cow Palace, Nov. 20, concert poster, 1973, U.S.

Quadrophenia press kit, with custom cover, eight typed pages on Track stationery, assorted black-and-white promo photos, 1973, U.S.

Quadrophenia tour program, black, orange, and blue graphics (there are also the lesser production "Fallout Shelter" and Show Souvenir programs used in the United States, plus a stand-alone program for the Charlton Athletic Club show), 1973, U.K.

"Love, Reign o'er Me" sheet music, black on pink with black-and-white live shot, $1.25, 1973, U.S.

"5:15" sheet music, blue ink, black-and-white shot of band, 20p, 1973, U.K.

"5:15"/"Water," black-and-white seated shot of band, Track, 1973, the Netherlands.

"5:15"/"Water," color live shot of band, Track, 1973, West Germany.

"5:15"/"Water," silver and black Track Records label showing through die-cut blue and yellow Fonica company sleeve, 1973, Guatemala.

"5:15"/"Water," silver and black Track Records label showing through die-cut blue, white, and black Polydor/Phonogram company sleeve, 1973, Malaysia.

"5:15"/"Love, Reign o'er Me," black and silver Track Records label showing through die-cut black-and-white International Polydor Production company sleeve, 1973, Greece.

"Love, Reign o'er Me"/"Is It in My Head?" monochrome blue band shot, 1973, the Netherlands.

"The Real Me"/"Water," *Quadrophenia* album cover shot, CBS/Sony, 1973, Japan.

"The Real Me"/"Doctor Jimmy," seven-inch, black and lavender ink, live shot, 1974, Belgium.

"Doctor [sic] Jimmy"/"The Real Me," black and yellow, band in rearview mirror graphic, 1974, France.

"Postcard"/"My Generation"/"Too Much of Anything"/"The Real Me," 33⅓ rpm seven-inch EP, color live shot of band, 1974, Brazil.

"Bellboy" tour book, featuring Keith dressed as a bellboy entering a hotel room to serve drinks, 1975, U.K.

Quadrophenia soundtrack album, withdrawn sleeve, given to cast and crew, 1979, U.K.

Quadrophenia soundtrack album, alternate front cover art featuring color shot of seven cast members (also available in Argentina with cropped version of alternate art—three cast members—on cassette), 1979, Argentina.

Quadrophenia soundtrack album, eight-track tape, in die-cut black and red Polydor sleeve, 1979, U.S.

Quadrophenia film and soundtrack promotional album, "Pete Townshend & Roger Daltrey talk about the Original Soundtrack Album and the forthcoming Who Film *Quadrophenia*, an exclusive interview banded and programmed for radio broadcast," 1979, U.S.

Quadrophenia film two-piece in-store mobile, 1979, U.S.

"5:15"/ "I'm One," seven-inch (issued in close to twenty versions around the world, about half with picture sleeves), 1979, Italy.

World-Northal Corporation and The Who Films Limited invite you to a sneak preview of the film *Quadrophenia*, 8th Street Playhouse hand bill, 1979, U.S.

Quadrophenia 8″x10″ color, promotional front-of-house still, on gloss, eight different, standard black-and-white exist as well, 1979, U.K.

Quadrophenia film poster using the art from the withdrawn album art, Polytel Film/Vesna Film, 1979, Yugoslavia.

Quadrophenia film poster, A Way of Life, 1979, U.K.

Quadrophenia cinema lobby standee, Polydor/film now on National release/Levi's, 1979, U.K.

Quadrophenia cinema lobby standee, die-cut picture of Jimmy on scooter, 1979, U.K.

Quadrophenia film program, *Quadrophenia*, A Way of Life, Levi's, Quality Never Goes Out of Style (there are also programs for Austria and Japan), 1979, U.K.

Quadrophenia soundtrack album, promo, alternate art with live shot, Polydor (there's also a second Mexican promo, with a black-and-white picture of the band and red text), 1980, Mexico.

Quadrophenia "A Condition of Today" one-sheet film poster, 1980, Australia.

Quadrophenia film poster, Les Who *Quadrophenia* 4 Players, pinball machine theme, 1980, France.

Quadrophenia film poster, with red and orange psychedelic typestyle for title (there are multiple variants), 1980, Italy.

Quadrophenia film on Beta Hi-fi (also issued in the U.K. with different cover art), 1981, U.S.

Quadrophenia soundtrack album, reissue with gold obi strip, 1982, Japan.

Quadrophenia soundtrack album, first CD pressing, white obi strip with black and red printing, 1991, Japan.

Quadrophenia film on LaserDisc (reissued in 1992 with different cover art), 1988, Japan.

Quadrophenia tour program, 1996, U.K.

Quadrophenia monochromatic green VIP Guest laminated backstage pass (also available in red, blue, and brown), 1996, U.K.

Quadrophenia, The Tour 2009, The Iconic Rock Opera, musical theatrical poster, 2009, U.K.

"Bell Boy," 45 rpm "picture disc" plastic postcard, made for many Who songs as well as other bands, with standard postcard pictures of flowers or landscapes, spindle hole in middle (these were also produced in 2011 for "Cut My Hair" and "Doctor Jimmy"), 2009, Poland.

The Who with Special Guest Vintage Trouble 11.12.2012, Target Center, Minneapolis, MN, tour poster, 2012, U.S.

Quadrophenia and More, 2012/13 North American tour program, 2012–2013, U.S.

Quadrophenia and More, 2012/13 North American tour VIP laminated backstage pass, 2012–2013, U.S.

discography

I've set this up as a list of highlights split into three categories. The first honors home soil for The Who, which in collecting terms—or book-collecting terms, at least—constitutes first edition or first issue. Then we've got American copies of *Quadrophenia*, with the United States constituting, somewhat, the most official (or at least prominent) issues. I've included a bit of color description (again, selectively) for extra distinction in the early days. Garden-variety reissues throughout the years have not been included. Finally, a miscellaneous section is included so we can scoop up any other interesting or historically significant versions of the album.

The most important years in the life of the album are 1973, when it was first issued; 1985, when it was first pressed to CD; 1996, when the first deluxe CD reissue took place, including the restored booklet; and 2011, when we got the massive director's cut box set, along with the more economical two-CD spin-off from the box.

U.K.			
LP	Track (black and silver)	2657 013	1973
Cassette	Track	3526 001	1973
8-Track	Track	3876 101	1973
CD (EU, made in Germany)	Polydor	831 074-2	1985
CD (EU, remixed, remastered)	Polydor	531 971-2	1996
LP (EU, 180 gm)	Polydor	831 074-1	2001
4 CD/1 DVD (EU, director's cut box set)	Polydor	2777840	2011
CD (EU, deluxe, second remix)	Polydor	2780503	2011
Blu-ray (EU)	Geffen	00602537808137	2014
LP (EU)	Polydor	2780504	2019
U.S.			
LP	Track/MCA (brown, silver, and blue)	MCA2-10004	1973
Cassette	Track/MCA	MCAC 2-6895	1973
Cassette	Track/MCA	MCAC2-10004	1973
8-Track	Track/MCA	MCAT2-10004	1973
Reel-to-Reel, 4 Track 7½ IPS	Track/MCA	MCAS 1004-K DP	1973
LP	MCA(rainbow logo)	MCA2-10004	1980
CD	MCA	MCAD2-6895	1985
CD, gold, remastered	Mobile Fidelity Sound Lab	UDCD 2-550	1991
CD, remixed, remastered	MCA	MCA 2-11463	1996
LP, 200 gm Quiex vinyl	Classic Records	2657 013	2007
CD, deluxe, second remix	Geffen	B0016090-02	2011
LP	Geffen	B0016090-01	2011

MISCELLANEOUS

LP, Canada	Track/MCA (black, silver, and blue)	MCA2-10004	1973
LP, Germany	Track (black and silver)	2409 203	1973
LP, France	Track/Polydor (black and silver)	2644 001	1973
LP, Italy	Track (red and white)	DTRL 34190	1973
LP, Israel	Litratone/Polydor (red and black)	2644 001	1973
LP, New Zealand	Track/Polydor (black and silver)	2657 013	1973
LP, Japan	Track (black and silver)	ECPI-1-TR	1973
LP, Japan	Track/CBS Sony (black and silver)	ECJ-9-TR	1973
Cassette, Germany	Track	3533 001	1973
Cassette, Italy	Track	34190-1	1973
LP, Brazil	Track/Phonogram	2409 203	1974
LP, Japan	CBS Sony (red and yellow)	40AP 1259	1979
CD, Japan	Polydor	POCP-2338/9	1994
CD, Japan (remixed, remastered)	Polydor	POCP-2526/27	1996
4 CD/1 DVD, Japan (director's cut box set)	Polydor	UICY-91798	2011
CD, Japan, deluxe, second remix	Polydor	UICY-10025/6	2011
CD (SACD), Japan	Polydor	UIGY-9597	2014

about the author

MARTIN POPOFF has unofficially written more record reviews—7,900, with over 7,000 appearing in his books—than anybody in the history of music writing across all genres. Popoff has penned approximately 120 books on hard rock, heavy metal, progressive rock, punk, classic rock, and record collecting. He was editor in chief of the now retired *Brave Words & Bloody Knuckles*, Canada's foremost heavy metal publication, for fourteen years and has also contributed to *Revolver, Guitar World, Goldmine, Record Collector*, Brave Words, Lollipop, and Hard Radio, with many record label band bios and liner notes to his credit as well. He has been a regular contractor to Banger Films, working for two years as researcher on the award-winning documentary *Rush: Beyond the Lighted Stage*, on the writing and research team for the eleven-episode *Metal Evolution* and the ten-episode *Rock Icons*, both for VH1 Classic. Additionally, Popoff is the writer of the original heavy metal genre chart used in *Metal: A Headbanger's Journey* and throughout the *Metal Evolution* episodes. He has solo-blabbed all over his own long-running audio podcast, *History in Five Songs with Martin Popoff*, for a number of years. He runs a YouTube channel with his buddy Marco D'Auria, called *The Contrarians* and is also a guest every Friday morning at 9:00 a.m. on Pete Pardo's *Sea of Tranquility* YouTube channel. Martin currently resides in Toronto and can be reached at martinp@inforamp.net or through www.martinpopoff.com.

image credits

A = all, L = left, M = middle, R = right, T = top

index

27 26 25 24 23   1 2 3 4 5

ISBN: 978-0-7603-7927-1

Digital edition published in 2023
eISBN: 978-0-7603-7928-8

Library of Congress Cataloging-in-Publication Data

Names: Popoff, Martin, 1963- author.
Title: The Who and Quadrophenia / Martin Popoff.
Description: Beverly : Motorbooks, 2023. | Includes index. | Summary: "The
    Who and Quadrophenia offers a generously illustrated deep dive into all
    aspects of one of the most popular rock albums of all time"-- Provided
    by publisher.
Identifiers: LCCN 2023006847 | ISBN 9780760379271 | ISBN 9780760379288
    (ebook)
Subjects: LCSH: Who (Musical group). Quadrophenia. | Rock
    music--1971-1980--History and criticism.
Classification: LCC ML421.W5 P66 2023 | DDC
    782.42166092/2--dc23/eng/20230419
LC record available at https://lccn.loc.gov/2023006847

Design: Cindy Samargia Laun
Front Cover Image: Pictorial Press Ltd/Alamy Stock Photo
Back Cover Image: Richard Kwasniewski via Frank White Photo Agency

Printed in China

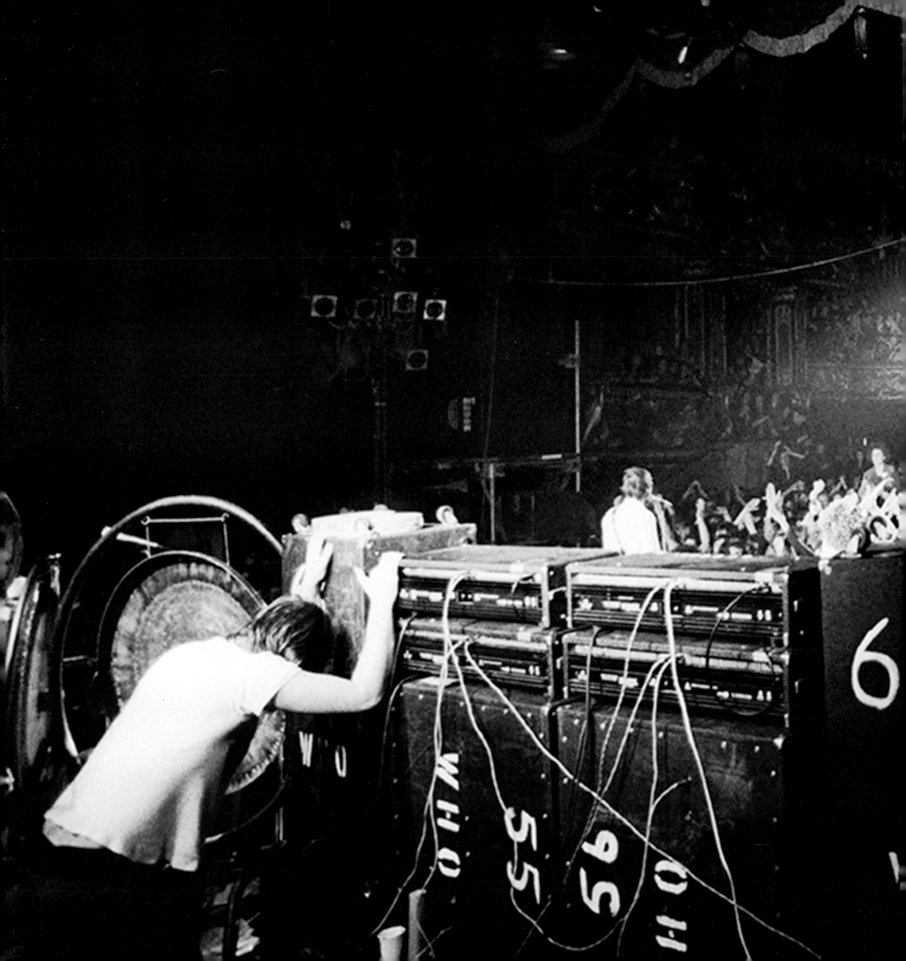